Bee Parables

⁓✣⁓

By

David M. Silk

Copyright © 2007 by David M. Silk

Bee Parables
by David M. Silk

Printed in the United States of America

ISBN 978-1-60266-219-3

All rights reserved solely by the author. The author guarantees all contents are original and do not infringe upon the legal rights of any other person or work. No part of this book may be reproduced in any form without the permission of the author. The views expressed in this book are not necessarily those of the publisher.

Unless otherwise indicated, Scripture quotations are taken from the New American Standard Bible ®, Copyright © 1960, 1962, 1963, 1968, 1971, 1972, 1973, 1975, 1977, 1995 by The Lockman Foundation. Used by permission.

Other Scripture quotations are from **The Message**. Copyright © by Eugene H. Peterson 1993, 1994, 1995, 1996, 2000, 2001, 2002. Used by permission of NavPress Publishing Group.

www.xulonpress.com

CONTENTS

Dedication vii
Acknowledgment ix

Chapter 1:   The Body and the Bees 11
Chapter 2:   The Basics of Bees 19
Chapter 3:   A Good Foundation 31
Chapter 4:   The Nursery 41
Chapter 5:   Cleaning House 53
Chapter 6:   Center of Attention 63
Chapter 7:   Drones 77
Chapter 8:   Communications 85
Chapter 9:   Personal Business 99
Chapter 10:   Guard Bees 105
Chapter 11:   Thieves 115
Chapter 12:   Belonging 127
Chapter 13:   Honey 139
Chapter 14:   Winter of the Soul 155
Chapter 15:   Mutiny 167
Chapter 16:   Smoke 173
Chapter 17:   Stuck on You 185
Chapter 18:   Influencing Your World 199
Chapter 19:   Multiplication by Division 211
Chapter 20:   Cutting Edge 223
Chapter 21:   Killer Bees 233
Chapter 22:   Being There 247
Chapter 23:   Navigation 269

Dedicated to Brenda - my wife,
my best friend and my honey

Acknowledgment

As you read through this book you will see how interdependent honeybees are with the rest of their hive-mates. The bees need each other. People also need each other.

As I reflect upon my life's journey I have to acknowledge that I am a product of my God-orchestrated past. The people with whom I have interacted along the way have contributed in some way to the person I am today. These people are family, friends, neighbors, teachers, pastors, professors, co-workers and even strangers. Some things I have incorporated into my life have been taught to me. Others were caught. Nevertheless I am grateful for the contribution, regardless of the quantity or the quality, from people too countless to name. My hope is that during my encounter with them I have in some way enriched their lives. I hope this book will be my way of saying thanks to everyone I have encountered on my journey as well as a way for me to contribute to others I have never met.

I would also like to acknowledge the sources that provided much of the factual and historical information about honeybees and beekeeping that are frequently cited in this book. For those who are interested in furthering their knowledge about honeybees the sources are as follows:

Starting Right with Bees: A Beginner's Handbook from The A. I. Root Company Publishers, 1976.

The New Complete Guide to Beekeeping by Roger A. Morse, The Countryman Press, 1994.

Honey Bee Biology and Beekeeping by Dewey M. Caron, Wicwas Press, 1999.

The Queen Must Die by William Longgood, W. W. Norton & Company, 1985.

I would also like to acknowledge Brushy Mountain Bee Farm Inc. for allowing me to use a few of their sketches to illustrate some aspects of the art of beekeeping.

Chapter 1

The Body and the Bees

About the time in life when children ask their parents for a pet—a cat, a dog or a goldfish—I asked my parents for a beehive. Being in a typical middle-class family with limited resources, I was used to having my requests denied due to budgetary restraints or safety concerns. "Can I get the latest battery-eating toy?" "No." "Can I get a cartoon-character wrist watch?" "No." "Can I get a model rocket kit and launch it inside the house?" "No."

It was in grade school that I acquired an interest in honeybees. If memory serves right, it was the *How and Why* science book series that introduced me to the world of social insects. I believe ants and termites were also mentioned in the book, but it was the honeybees that piqued my interest. I remember marveling at the close-up pictures and wondering how anyone could get so close to all of those stinging bees. I was also fascinated that the scientists who studied the honeybees could know so much about them. The book went on to describe how every bee (except for the lazy drones) would busily perform their job that, in a small way, contributed to the overall well being and continuation of the colony.

I was hooked (or maybe a more appropriate term was I got the "bug"). After immersing myself in all the information I could find about honeybees, I was still very intrigued by these creatures. By this time I had learned ordinary people could keep bees with only a small investment of time and equipment. Therefore it seemed logical that the next step for me to continue to grow in this area was to become a beekeeper myself.

"Can I get a beehive?" "OK."

"OK????!" I must admit I was shocked by my parents' response and briefly wondered if aliens had taken over their bodies. In hindsight I now realize timing has a lot to do with how parents respond to their children's requests. In my case, my request came about the time that our family had bought a six-acre gentleman's farm complete with various fruit trees. It was also surrounded by hundreds of acres of farmland with all kinds of blossoming foliage. My mother had grown up on a nearby farm and was well aware of the benefits of having bees to pollinate crops and fruit trees. Since her parents had lived through the Great Depression, she had learned from them about using honey as a sweetener when sugar was not always readily available. My father probably shared my interest in bees and used me as an excuse to indulge his curiosity. But after we started harvesting honey he liked the idea of making a few extra bucks by selling honey to his co-workers.

"OK"—now what? Being about eleven years old I did not have a clue as to how to proceed. But my father stepped in and contacted an acquaintance of his who was a veteran beekeeper. Once we purchased the basic equipment—a beekeeper's veil, a pair of protective gloves, a device to make smoke and a small crowbar-type tool with a sharp flat edge—this veteran beekeeper brought some bees in a small hive (comprised of one box or "super," as it is called) to our farm. Whether my father paid this man for the hive or he did it out of the goodness of his heart I will never know. All I knew was that I was about to experience firsthand what I had only seen in textbooks.

This gentleman gave me some pointers as we prepared to enter the hive. He instructed me to tuck my pant cuffs down into my socks to prevent bees from crawling up my legs. I also tucked my long-sleeved jacket into my pants. I then donned my veil and secured it tightly around my torso. Lastly I put on the long protective gloves that went up to my elbows. My father made sure no part of me was exposed because, with all of the clothing that needed to be properly arranged, there was always the possibility of a small opening to exist for the bees to enter.

This acquaintance of my father was an elderly man who had kept bees for many years. I do not recall much this veteran beekeeper said that day, but I do remember he was not wearing gloves. (Later I learned that most serious beekeepers do not wear gloves for a variety of reasons.) Now the big moment came. Theory met reality and I was in the middle. We puffed smoke into the hive entrance and waited a few moments. As we opened the hive by lifting its roof, some bees started flying around us. Soon I and my mentor were immersed in a small cloud of bees. Nothing I had read described or prepared me for what I was experiencing. It was very unnerving to hear bees buzzing around my head. I remember being on the verge of panic and thought I was going to drop everything and run away screaming. But at that same time I remembered I was wearing protective gear. Was I going to succumb to fear and forsake my passion or was I going to trust my gear and proceed? The right side of my brain said, "Don't you hear all of those bees? Run!" The left side of my brain said, "Stay. You're safe."

To this day that moment in my life has been the best illustration of walking by faith. The choice of living by fear or facts is always before us. Do we allow our feelings to dictate our course of action, or do we resolve to adhere to that which we know to be true? Faith is much more than a feeling. It is a deep-seated trust in God.

Despite the cloud of bees circling about my head, I stood next to this gentleman and watched as he gently pulled out a few frames from the box and inspected each one. He let me do the same with a few frames. He pointed out various things, but my mind was not focused on him or his words. After having conquered my fear, I was completely enthralled in the experience and could not believe I was actually in a hive of bees! When we finished the inspection, I helped him close the hive, and we walked to where my father stood nearby observing us. This seasoned beekeeper turned to my father and said, "He'll be a good beekeeper—he's not afraid."

What a vote of confidence! Obviously he was not privy to my right-brain/left-brain debate. But his kind words of affirmation touched my heart and launched me into the hobby of beekeeping with a sense of confidence. Throughout our lives we interact with thousands of people and, unfortunately, most of our conversations with these people are just mundane words that are soon forgotten. But well-measured and properly timed words from others are treasured and can have an immeasurable impact. As you are reading this, I hope you can recall the times you have been the recipient of such kind words.

Kind words which provide encouragement and comfort usually do not just drop from the sky. They come from other people. Christians are part of God's kingdom community. These community members are supposed to work together. The apostle Paul illustrated this beautifully in 1 Corinthians 12 in his discussion on the use of spiritual gifts (such as, teaching, serving, and administrating) among the members of the Corinthian church. This chapter of the Bible tells us these gifts are not for individual benefit but individuals are to apply them within a unified body of believers because the same Spirit is the sovereign provider of the gifts.[1] Paul, like any good teacher, used imagery familiar to his audience to convey the idea that the well-being of individuals depended upon the well-being of the group. This imagery had been used in ancient times before Paul by Socrates, Aristotle and the Roman Consul

Menenius Agrippa and during Paul's lifetime by the Roman playwright Seneca.[2]

In 1 Corinthians 12 the various members of Christ's church are likened to parts of the human body. Every part is different, but the parts are to work together. Each member is to be satisfied with his or her role and is expected to make a contribution to the good of the community. Visibility or appearances are not what matter. This is true with respect to the physical body as well as to a church. The internal organs, protected and hidden from view, are essential to life. Similarly, there are "invisible" members in every church that are likewise essential to its survival and operation. God in His sovereignty distributes the spiritual gifts among believers and orchestrates the various members of the church body for the common good. Paul encourages all believers, regardless of apparent importance, to work together in a spirit of unity.

Unity's odd partner is diversity. Every one is different, but each has an important part to play. A church could not function if all of its members had similar gifts just as a sports team would not be successful if its entire roster was comprised of individuals skilled in only one of the many positions. Paul wrote about unity amidst diversity. Each member is unique and uniquely gifted. Therefore each believer must identify and use his or her gifts. When trying to identify our gifts we should take note of the fact that the lists of spiritual gifts that are provided in the New Testament are not identical. Perhaps God distributed specific gifts among the people at different churches based upon their unique needs or circumstances.

That being the case, we should be somewhat broad minded as we assess the giftedness of ourselves and others, especially in light of a special need or situation at any given church.[3]

However, Christianity has largely become a spectator sport as much of the laity watches the professional Christians do most of the work. One Bible commentator believes there are many undiscovered and unused gifts.[4] Why is so much unused potential just sitting in the pews? After the fall of man in the Garden of Eden, mankind has wanted to become independent of God. It was only a short step before this attitude of independence found its way into human relationships as well and thus the source of individualism that permeates our culture today.[5]

An individual honeybee literally cannot live for more than about one day separated from its colony. Also, because of the simultaneous tasks being performed by individual members, honeybees are inescapably interdependent upon one another such that some have suggested the whole colony should be considered as a single organism.[6]

Whenever I read 1 Corinthians 12, I am reminded of how a honeybee colony functions. Entomologists (those who study insects) have been able to identify numerous tasks that are performed every day by the members of a honeybee colony. Although more than sixty thousand individual bees may be in a hive, they all work together for the common good. Somehow their efforts are coordinated with amazing efficiency to the benefit of all the members. They are so successful that we humans also reap huge benefits from these tiny creatures. Likewise, though, if there is a disruption or problem within the hive, the entire colony will feel the effect. Depending upon the problem, it could be a setback or even fatal to the colony. Similarly, positive and negative results will occur within a church depending upon the degree of mutual support and cooperation that exists among it members.

This is not another book about spiritual gifts. It should be pointed out, however, that wherever the spiritual gifts are listed in the New Testament (Romans 12:3-8, 1 Corinthians 12:28-31, Ephesians 4:7-11 and 1 Peter 4:10-11) there are purposes stated for the gifts (Romans 12:6; 1 Corinthians 12:7, 25; Ephesians 4:12-14; and 1 Peter 4:10). In short, the spiritual gifts are to be used to build up those within the church. Therefore, the purpose of this book is to encourage believers to be active within a church community as a contributor as well as a recipient just as is done within a colony of bees. Thus, while exploring different aspects and acts of cooperation that occur within the honeybee world, each chapter will seek to encourage a parallel response between members within the body of Christ.

I hope readers will enjoy learning something about honeybees. But the major intent of the subsequent chapters is to help believers realize their importance within God's family and how vitally important it is to them.

Chapter 2

The Basics of Bees

In order for someone to make better sense of the parallels between the workings of believers within the church and the activities in the honeybee world, a brief overview of the basic concepts of honeybees and beekeeping is in order. I hope this overview will not be too short, thus leaving out important details, or too technical, thereby introducing confusion to the subject.

To start off, it is interesting to know that honeybees are not native to North America. The colonists brought honeybees with them from Europe in the 1600s. Since the time of their introduction, honeybees spread throughout the continent by swarming—a natural process of propagating the species. Despite being foreigners to the continent, honeybees became well established. In North America today there are about one hundred thousand beekeepers[1]—the vast majority being hobbyists—and there are about 2.5 million honeybee colonies rented annually in the United States for crop pollination.[2] So whether the bees are kept by hobbyists or used for big business today, it is interesting to note that a few centuries earlier in Europe families practiced "telling the bees" — when a black cloth was placed on a hive to signify to the bees their owner had died.[3]

Three different types of bees comprise a colony. First is the queen bee. Usually only one is in a colony at any given time. Her main job is to lay eggs. She can lay between one and two thousand eggs per day! Her name, obviously, is associated with royalty, and therefore one might be inclined to think the queen bee has authority over the activities of the colony. But it is believed the queen may not be in charge although she is the single most important member of the colony. She does, however, emit pheromones, or special scents, that somehow provide the colony with a sense of identity and maintain social order within the colony. Predominantly she is simply a very specialized worker—an egg-laying machine. Queen bees can live for several years but lose their effectiveness with age.

Every year commercial beekeepers usually replace the queens in their hives with younger ones. This is done because younger queen bees generally are better egg layers. The more eggs laid mean more bees. More bees will translate into a stronger work force. A stronger work force means more honey can be harvested and thus the underlying logic and economics behind commercial beekeeping. So, one might ask, "Where can the commercial beekeepers get new queen bees?" They can either raise new queens themselves, or they can order them from apiaries in the southern United States that specialize in supplying bees (queens and workers) for beekeepers. It is beyond the scope of this book to explain how queen bees are commercially raised. It is just another one of the fascinating aspects of the beekeeping world.

Queen bees can actually choose to lay one of two types of eggs—fertilized or unfertilized. Worker bees, which comprise the vast majority of the colony's population, develop from fertilized eggs. Workers are female bees with underdeveloped ovaries and cannot breed. But worker bees perform a variety of tasks as members of the colony. These tasks include nursery duty, hive cleaning, making wax, scouting, foraging, guarding and tending the queen. Amazingly these and other activities are performed simultaneously and harmoniously by thousands of bees for the overall well-being of the colony.

Laying over one thousand eggs per day sounds like a recipe for overpopulation. During the warm season of the year, though, when the bees do most of their work they only live a short time. Estimates of their life span during the warmer months range from four to eight weeks. Their life span is short because they literally work themselves to death. There is much work to be done to support the colony on a daily basis as well as to prepare for the upcoming winter. To do all of the required chores, one can see why there can be sixty thousand worker bees or more in a single colony during its peak. During the winter months when the bees are not working as hard, they can live up to six months. But the queen will stop laying eggs for a brief period in the early winter. When she resumes egg laying, she does so at a reduced rate. Therefore by spring the hive population will shrink to about twenty thousand or less before climbing again when the rising temperatures of spring bring about fresh food supplies that prompt increased egg laying.

Drones, the male member of the species, develop from an unfertilized egg. It seems contrary to basic biology that an unfertilized egg would develop into in a mature bee. For those interested in scientific terminology, the process by which drones develop from unfertilized eggs is called parthenogenesis or haplodiploidy.[4] There may be between several hundred and a few thousand drones in a healthy colony. Drones do two things in life—eat and try to mate. They do nothing else. They do not clean up. They do not help with the rearing of the developing baby bees (called brood). They do not gather food. They do not even have a stinger with which to protect themselves or the other members of the colony. In fact, they do not even feed themselves! Worker bees must stop what they are doing to feed these free-loaders. For the most part the drones have it pretty good. But their fate dramatically changes as cold weather approaches in the fall.

The place where the bees reside is called the hive. (As a side note, beekeepers may use the terms *hive* or *colony* interchangeably when referring to their bees.) The hive can be located inside a hollow tree, in an attic, in the wall space of a building or in those white boxes located along the edge of a country field. Hives can exist in rural as well as urban settings. I can remember visiting my grandparents' farm over the years and seeing honeybees coming and going from the trunk of a large maple tree. One beekeeper recounted the story of being contracted to remove honeybees from the attic of a museum. After capturing and removing the bees, the beekeeper was assigned the task of removing the wax comb and their contents from the attic. All told, several hundred pounds of honey were removed! Obviously, if the wax comb detached from the attic rafters, it could have fallen through the thin attic floor and damaged the museum pieces below. (If it was an art museum, then surely an art critic would have tried to interpret the gooey mess as an abstract work reflecting some aspect of the human condition!) Another beekeeper recently claimed that there are more colonies of bees living within wall spaces of buildings in a major city than exist in the surrounding suburban counties. But as far as a hive location goes, bees will set up shop any place that is dry, clean and easily defendable.

Before today's hive boxes were developed, bees were kept in what was called a skep. A skep looked like an upside down woven basket. To extract the honey the bees were removed from the skep. The comb was torn out of the skep, and the honey was collected. This process was very inefficient as the wax comb containing honey (and brood) was destroyed. To start the process over, bees would be reintroduced to the skep and would rebuild the comb to have a place to rear brood and store honey. It takes the bees quite a bit of energy (honey) to build new comb. Furthermore, the time required to build new comb could otherwise be used to gather nectar and make more honey. Another drawback to the skep was that beekeepers were unable to inspect the bees to determine their general condition or to check for the presence of diseases.

The modern beehive came about due to the close observations of Reverend L. L. Langstroth in 1851.[5] These observations focused on the natural spacing honeybees use in constructing their wax combs in the wild. This natural spacing was incorporated into the hive structure. If the spacing is too small or too large, the bees will build wax bridges or burr (excess and un-useful) comb to fill the space. Thus, when the modern hive boxes were designed, this spacing was a key factor to minimize burr comb and make the bees feel more at home.

Hive boxes (called supers) are designed to be stacked one upon another. They are added as the colony grows and space is needed to store excess honey. (See Figure 1 for an exploded view of a beehive.) The supers typically come in two sizes. The larger ones are called brood boxes because they are where the bees will raise their brood. The brood boxes are usually on the bottom of the stack of supers. The smaller supers are generally used by beekeepers to collect excess honey, and they are on top of the stack. Bees have a natural tendency when storing honey to start at the top of the hive and work downward. The queen, on the other hand, will generally work upward as she lays eggs. By taking advantage of this behavior the beekeeper can easily remove the top boxes to extract the honey without disrupting or destroying the brood. Some beekeepers, however,

Bee Parables

use a wire mesh called a "queen excluder" to keep the queen in the bottom part of the hive so the honey and brood will remain separated.

The smaller supers will weigh about fifty pounds when full of honey. This is not a light load to be lifting. But it is preferred over the eighty pounds a full brood box weighs! (Beekeepers try to work smarter not harder.) Furthermore, the beekeeper will not disturb the honey in the brood boxes. This honey will be the food the bees will use to survive the coming winter.

Also included in the hive design was the capability to readily inspect the bees while inflicting little damage to the wax comb and minimal loss of life to the bees. Inside the supers are removable frames. The frames hang vertically from ledges near the tops of the supers. Within the rectangular outline of the frames the bees build their wax comb. The frames can be easily withdrawn for inspection or replacement if necessary. When it comes time to harvest the honey, beekeepers will remove the frames that are filled with honey. The wax cappings are cut or scraped off from the sealed honeycomb. The frames are then placed in a centrifuge where they are spun. The spinning action will cause the honey to come out of the comb and will be collected at the bottom of the centrifuge tank. The emptied frames are then placed back in the supers. The supers are put back on the hive for the bees to refill.

The hive has a base, called a "bottom board," which supports the supers. The bottom board is actually a tray that extends out from under the bottom super to provide a landing area and entrance to the hive. Beekeepers will adjust the entrance size based upon the strength of the colony and ventilation needs. A weak colony can better defend a smaller entrance. In the summer a larger entrance helps the bees to ventilate the hive better to keep it cool and to dry (or ripen) the honey. In winter the entrance is closed except for a very small opening to keep rodents out while allowing some air to enter the hive for the bees to breath.

The roof of the hive is called the top cover. The top cover has a lip around its edge that will fit around the outside of the top of the highest super. This lip functions to secure the top cover to the hive. Many beekeepers will place rocks or bricks on the top covers to keep them from being blown off by the wind. The top cover simply rests atop the uppermost super and is the finishing piece to the stacked supers.

The stacking feature of these components allows for easy disassembly and reassembly of the hive by the beekeeper. When going into the hive, the top cover is the first piece that is removed. It will be laid upside down next to the hive. After inspecting the highest super, the beekeeper will remove that super from the hive and stack it on the upside-down top cover at a ninety-degree angle. Setting the super on the upside-down top cover prevents laying the super directly on the ground and thus coming in contact with dirt or debris. The next super removed from the hive will be placed on top of the top super (now resting on the top cover) at a ninety-degree angle. (The ninety-degree angle offset makes it easier to pick up the supers when they are reassembled back onto the hive.) This process continues until the inspection is completed. Thus, the top cover serves not only as a roof for the hive but as a foundation for supers that are temporarily removed from the hive.

Bees do most of their work during the warm months. During the winter, things slow down, but the bees do not hibernate. They huddle, or cluster, and basically do aerobics to generate heat to keep warm. They tap into their stored honey and pollen to eat during the winter and to feed the developing brood. For the brood to develop it must be about 94° F.[6] Somehow in the midst of a frigid winter the bees manage to maintain this temperature at the core of their huddle. The bees rotate from the interior of the cluster to the exterior and back again so that each member can be warmed and thus not freeze by remaining too long on the exterior of the cluster.

I hope this brief introduction to bees has been informative and has whetted your intellectual appetite for more details about their world. They are indeed fascinating creatures. Their collective teamwork has intrigued human beings for centuries. They are very ordered and highly efficient as they methodically go about their business for the collective good. Their complex social structure rivals that of mankind. They work so well together and are so interdependent that some have made the case that the entire colony should be considered a single organism.

The Christian church can learn a lot about functioning as a community by observing the honeybee. The bees are living parables. It is hoped the remaining chapters will successfully explain the details of how bees work together as a community. May this be an encouragement to Christians everywhere to become more deeply involved and integrated with their spiritual brothers and sisters in a local body of believers.

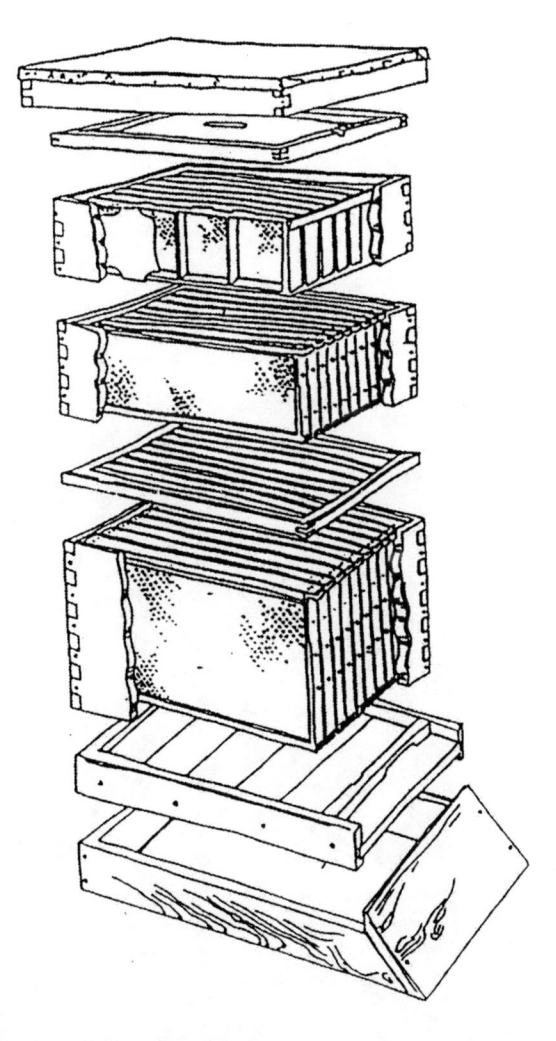

Figure 1: An Exploded View of a Beehive. From the top down: top cover, inner cover, two shallow supers, a queen excluder, a brood box, bottom board and base. (Courtesy of Brushy Mountain Bee Farm Inc.)

Chapter 3

A Good Foundation

Wax is an essential honeybee product used in the construction of a hive. Bees have several pairs of glands on the underside of their abdomens that secrete wax. Younger bees have more capability to produce this substance than older bees. When a bee secretes wax, another bee will gather the substance and use it in some kind of construction project. The main use bees have for wax is to build the hexagonal-shaped cells. These cells are used as storage bins for honey and pollen and are also used for cradling future generations of bees. Bees also use wax is as a lid on the cells which contain honey and as a thin curtain for the larvae in their final stage of development within the cells. The bees can recycle their wax if necessary. Overall, beeswax is a pliable but sturdy substance and therefore suits the bees' purposes perfectly.

There are a few things that can threaten the wax besides the brute force of a beekeeper or a bear. One of those threats is heat. Beeswax has a melting point of about 144° F.[1] During the hot summer months, as the external temperature rises, the wax may begin to soften. Depending upon a hive's exposure to the sun (especially in a hot climate), the combs can melt from the heat.[2] But the bees can control the temperature of the hive. They do this by bringing water into the hive and spreading it around on the wax surfaces. Then, by fanning their wings, they create air flow through the hive. This evaporates the water and cools the hive. Therefore it is necessary for the bees to have a local water supply for both individual hydration and for cooling the hive. If the wax combs have a meltdown and collapse it will be a mess and the bees will probably abandon the hive. One reason why beekeepers, especially in warmer climates, paint their hives white is to help keep the beehives cool in the summer because light colors reflect heat whereas darker colors absorb heat. In cooler northern climates the opposite is true as beekeepers may paint their hives a darker color to help the bees keep the hive warm, especially during the winter and early spring.

Beeswax is comprised of over three hundred different ingredients—none comprising more than eight percent of the total mixture.[3] Despite this knowledge, it has not been replicated by scientists. Wax's unique combination of ingredients combine to instill qualities that can preserve it for centuries as it has been found in the tombs of ancient Egypt.[4]

Honeybees are terrific engineers as they use this unique substance effectively. It has been said that of all the symmetrical shapes to use in building a structure of repetitive shapes, none is sturdier than the hexagon. The strong hexagonal-shaped cells also afford the bees a way of storing the most amount of honey with a minimal amount of wax. Although the cell walls are less than one one-thousandth of an inch in thickness, the comb is constructed such that one pound of beeswax can hold twenty-two pounds of honey.[5] Given its design and durability, it is not surprising that wax comb has been known to endure the wear and tear of repeated use within a hive for up to forty years.[6]

Although the bees that originally supplied the wax and built the comb live only a few weeks, they provide a lasting legacy that serves countless future generations of bees. Christians can also leave a lasting legacy in the world. Three things last forever—God, His Word and men's souls. Although we can have no impact on these first two, we can influence people. It is an incredible thought that we can impact future generations by simply being faithful to advance God's kingdom today. This long-lasting impact can come about through our posterity as we lay a foundation in the lives of others.

The apostle Paul used the *foundation* metaphor in several of his epistles. Paul told the believers in Ephesus how they got to their state of spiritual well being. "So then you are no longer strangers and aliens, but you are fellow citizens with the saints, and are of God's household, *having been built on the foundation of the apostles and prophets*, Christ Jesus Himself being the corner stone, in whom the whole building, being fitted together, is growing into a holy temple in the Lord, in whom you also are being built together into a dwelling of God in the Spirit" (Ephesians 2:19-22).

Paul cautioned the rich to invest with an eternal mindset. "Instruct those who are rich in this present world not to be conceited or to fix their hope on the uncertainty of riches, but on God, who richly supplies us with all things to enjoy. Instruct them to do good, to be rich in good works, to be generous and ready to share, *storing up for themselves the treasure of a good foundation* for the future, so that they may take hold of that which is life indeed" (1 Timothy 6:17-19).

In referring to the earning of rewards on judgment day, Paul wrote, "According to the grace of God which was given to me, like a wise master builder *I laid a foundation*, and another is building on it. But each man must be careful how he builds on it. For no man can lay a foundation other than the one which is laid, which is Jesus Christ. Now if any man builds on the foundation with gold, silver, precious stones, wood, hay, straw, each man's work will become evident; for the day will show it because it is to be revealed with fire, and the fire itself will test the quality of each man's work. If any man's work which he has built on it remains, he will receive a reward. If any man's work is burned up, he will suffer loss; but he himself will be saved, yet so as through fire" (1 Corinthians 3:10-15).

Although Peter did not use the *foundation* metaphor for church growth, he did mention how the Old Testament prophets were on a mission to impact future generations while they themselves were not told how things would unfold. "As to this salvation, the prophets who prophesied of the grace that would come to you made careful searches and inquiries, seeking to know what person or time the Spirit of Christ within them was indicating as He predicted the sufferings of Christ and the glories to follow. *It was revealed to them that they were not serving themselves, but you,* in these things which now have been announced to you through those who preached the gospel to you by the Holy Spirit sent from heaven—things into which angels long to look" (1 Peter 1:10-12).

Some might think these verses express grandiose ideas that applied only to the apostles or to special men and women of God. But the principle of living with an eternal perspective applies to all believers. Jesus said, "Do not store up for yourselves treasures on earth, where moth and rust destroy, and where thieves break in and steal. But store up for yourselves treasures in heaven, where neither moth nor rust destroys, and where thieves do not break in or steal; for where your treasure is, there your heart will be also" (Matthew 6:19-21). So what is your treasure and where is your heart?

We all get caught up in the here-and-now. Jobs, school, marriage, kids, church, home maintenance, vacation, elderly parents, community service, soccer games and the like. It is easy to think temporally rather than eternally. None of us can see heaven; but we can see the world around us, and of course it is easier to address what is seen than what is not seen. Most believers have good intentions of serving God in a greater capacity. But they delay taking action thinking a better time of service will come later. The truth is that "later" never comes as there will always be unique demands on our time in each stage of our lives. The present will always try to seduce us with things that are urgent to distract us from things which are eternal.

To help acquire an eternal perspective, take a long quiet thoughtful walk through a cemetery.

During the summers of my high school years I worked in the town cemetery. At first this may sound a bit creepy, but all in all it was not a bad job for a high school student. When my buddies and I got together and discussed our summer jobs I always had the best lines. After they talked about their jobs I would speak about mine and say, "People are just dying to get in there," or "Where I work I have twenty thousand people under me." Pardon the cemetery humor.

My duties at the cemetery entailed periodically running a weed-whacker to trim headstones for the Memorial Day and Fourth of July holidays. Following funerals, when the caskets had been lowered into the ground, a co-worker and I would fill in the graves to bury the deceased. All told, in four summers I had participated in burying twenty-eight people. Several weeks after the ground settled we would return to the grave site and pour a concrete base for a headstone. But by far most of my many hours in the cemetery were spent walking behind a self-propelled mower between the seemingly endless rows of headstones. No sooner had we finished mowing the entire cemetery than it was time to start all over again.

While I walked behind a mower, the hum of the engine would block out the rest of the world. During this state of isolation it was easy to get lost in my thoughts. Many times I found myself simply reading the headstones as I walked by. Some would have a witty line or term of endearment. But for the most part there were only names and dates. I would find myself doing quick arithmetic in my head to calculate the age of people when they had died. After a while I noticed there was no apparent rhyme or reason for the age of someone at death. Some folks lived to a ripe old age while others died as infants, and of course there were all those in between. Some had died recently while others had died in the past and their life span had briefly overlapped mine. Many had died before I was born. Others had been dead so long that no person alive had any firsthand knowledge of the deceased. Still others had been dead so long the elements had eroded the headstones and made the inscriptions unreadable.

For me as a young person this experience significantly reinforced the concept of the inevitability of death. Every one of us will face it, and we can face it during any season of our lives. The realization of the shortness of life on earth and the significance of eternity is no more powerful than in a cemetery. I am sure the people buried in every cemetery had at one time been busy living their lives. They had jobs, family, community and personal interests that demanded their time and attention. The further back into history we look, we realize simple survival was almost a full-time effort that consumed the time of individuals, families and communities. In any case, those who have lived before us are here no longer.

Their busy lives were no more than mere dots on the endless timeline of eternity.

When we reflect upon the activities of our predecessors, we see that many of the things which consumed their time are no longer here either. The family farm is now a housing development. The factory building has been torn down, and its jobs have now been outsourced to another country. Advanced degrees do nothing for the dead. Accumulated wealth has been dispersed to those who did not earn it. The once prized items from hobbies or personal interests are now items for sale at flee markets. Friends and family members have moved or passed away. The point is that nothing is permanent. All the things of this world will eventually turn to dust.

How do you make an eternal difference? First, invest in people. Be their friend. Hang out with nonbelievers and believers alike. Opportunities abound—ball games, shows, walks, meals—to share each other's life story and experiences. Listen carefully. Let the uniqueness of every person enrich your life. It is hoped that amidst your friendship they will notice the various aspects of your life. If Christ is a significant part of your life, then it should be evident, and spiritual things should become a natural topic of discussion. When the discussion touches upon spiritual matters, be honest and genuine as you relate your faith journey with your friends. Share the good and the bad, but point out how Jesus has made the difference in your life. Encourage nonbelievers to consider the claims of Jesus and encourage believers to continue on with their relationship with

Him. When life is over, the decisions that will matter most are those regarding how individuals respond to Jesus. Discussing spiritual things can sometimes be a challenge. Be patient. People do remember and process what is said from a person they perceive as a concerned friend.

Second, ask yourself, "What does my checkbook say about my priorities?" When police are investigating potential suspects they follow the money trail. How you spend your money says a lot about you. What do you do with your discretionary money? Do you own your possessions, or do they own you? Are you a faithful steward of all God has given you? This is not a hint that believers are to live a Spartan lifestyle and must give everything away to God's work. There is nothing wrong with wealth in and of itself. On the other hand, neither is poverty an absolute sign of piety. The key is to surrender your resources, regardless of the amount, to God and respond to His leading. Wealth can be a tremendous force for good in the world and can be used to advance God's kingdom. For example, it was been said that a few dollars can be used to buy a Bible and send it to a third-world country where Bibles are scarce. One report indicated that, unlike in this country where Bibles abound and largely go unused, a single Bible in some areas of the world will be actively circulated and used by as many as fifty people. Isn't a small sacrifice on our part worth the eternal impact in the lives of others?

Life is short, and it can be morbid if one dwells on the thought of death. But Christians have a joyful hope beyond the grave. They also have a tremendous opportunity and responsibility to play a part in conveying this message of hope to others. In so doing, one can invest in something that will not turn to dust. Things we do now can impact eternity. Laying a foundation now will benefit countless others in the future. Consider your own spiritual heritage for a moment. Someone shared the gospel with you. Someone had shared the gospel with the one who shared it with you. Thus, each believer is the result of a long legacy of evangelists that ultimately began with Christ and the apostles.

Keep the legacy going! Follow the example of the honeybee and build something that will outlast you. Let your life be a foundation that will benefit those who come after you. Listen to Paul's words: "The things which you have heard from me in the presence of many witnesses, entrust these to faithful men *who will be able to teach others also*" (2 Timothy 2:2). Do not let your headstone be the end of the line.

Chapter 4

The Nursery

When one thinks of honeybees, the next thought is usually about honey. So when someone sees a beehive in the corner of a field, they immediately recognize it as such and then think of honey. However, a beehive is first and foremost an incubator for developing bees and then secondly a storage facility for honey.

In order for a colony to gather and store honey, it first must have a large workforce. Whenever a new colony is getting started, the first order of business is to build the wax comb which contains the many thousands of hexagonal cells that will cradle future generations of worker bees. Once the cells are built, the queen—an egg-laying machine—will carefully deposit eggs into the cells. She is capable of laying one to two thousand eggs per day! Why so many? During the active season the workers only live about six weeks. With such a short life span and with so much to do, the work force needs to be large and constantly replenished.

The time from when **the queen** lays a worker-bee egg to the time it emerges **as a mature** bee is twenty-one days. Assuming a **life span of** six weeks for the worker bees and assuming **the queen** lays one thousand eggs per day, the **population** of a newly started colony will peak at about **fifty-two** thousand in about nine weeks when the **number of** emerging mature bees approximately equals the number of bees that die. This is a rough estimate. The queen may lay differing amounts of eggs from one day to the next. Some bees may live longer than six weeks while others will live less. A range of fifty to sixty thousand is a good guess for any given colony at full strength which occurs around the beginning of summer.

Why so many bees? The ultimate goal is the survival of the colony. To accomplish this, the bees not only have to feed and care for themselves on a daily basis, but they also must feed the developing young as well as gather and store food for survival through the upcoming winter season. Each bee will produce about one twelfth of an ounce of honey during its short lifetime. By itself this amount is almost meaningless. But multiplying it ten thousand times or so is significant and vital for the future food supply of the colony. Thus, with survival as the ultimate goal and with food as the obvious necessity, a strong population of worker bees is vital to the continuation of the colony. Hence, a beehive is first and foremost a place to lay eggs and develop them into mature worker bees.

The development of mature workers is a complex and cooperative effort. As was stated above, the comb and the cells must first be built. This employs bees to make the wax and others to mold it into shape. Once built, the queen will deposit the eggs into the cells. If there is no need to build new comb, housecleaning bees will clean previously used cells and prepare them to receive the eggs. When an egg hatches, it is then called a larva. The larva will develop and go through the pupa stage before it emerges as a mature adult worker bee.

During these stages of development the larvae must be tended. Nurse bees assume this responsibility. Being a nurse is one of the first tasks a bee performs in its life. For about three days after the eggs hatch, worker-bee larvae are only fed royal jelly. Royal jelly is secreted from glands located on the heads of young nurse bees. These nurse bees can only produce this nutrient-rich substance during the first few days of their life. After this phase of their life, these "old" nurse bees graduate and move on to their next assignment as they are replaced by younger nurses. Just like beeswax, this unique food substance cannot be reproduced by science either. This substance is so unique that no waste is generated by the larvae that consume it.[1]

After the first three days the larvae are fed a combination of honey and pollen. As a rule-of-thumb it takes about one cell of honey and one cell of pollen to feed each larva during its development.[2] During the entire developmental process each of the larvae is tended for various reasons about ten thousand times by nurse bees up to and including the capping of their cells.[3] Under this thin curtain of wax the final stage of growth and transformation occurs until the mature bee emerges.

Another fascinating aspect of this developmental process is temperature control. By controlling the internal temperature the bees essentially turn the hive into an incubator. In order for this process to occur properly, the eggs, larvae and pupae (collectively referred to as brood) must be maintained at approximately 94° F. To generate and maintain this temperature the bees gather around the brood area. Their collective body heat generates the necessary energy. Their clustered bodies also act as insulation to keep the warmth in and the cold out.

This may not seem too difficult for the bees to do during the summertime. In fact, being too hot is a concern during the warmer months. But regardless of the season of the year the bees will maintain the necessary temperature whenever there is brood in the hive. In northern states the queen will stop laying eggs between late November and early January. When the queen resumes laying eggs (perhaps associated with the lengthening of the daylight hours[4]), the bees will cluster in such a way that, despite frigid external temperatures, the brood will develop to become mature worker bees ready for spring chores. During the winter the bees will rotate from the inside of the cluster to the outside so that no bees remain on the outside of the cluster and freeze. The bees will feed themselves and the developing brood with pollen and honey stored during the warm months by their now long-dead predecessors.

Beekeepers should inspect their hives throughout the year including the winter and early spring season. Inspections during colder seasons should be as brief as possible. If the beekeeper takes too long during colder months, he runs the risk of "chilling" the brood. If that occurs, the developing larvae will die. The bees will then have to waste time and energy to remove the dead larvae. Furthermore, the loss of developing brood during the late winter and early spring is a major setback for the colony. Every bee is needed during this time of the year to help the colony grow as fast as possible to be able to be in the best possible condition to take full advantage of the peak nectar flow in early summer.

Honeybees, like any creature, are fighting for survival. They fight this war collectively with the major battle being waged inside the hive by raising the next generation of bees. With a sufficient work force many important functions can be performed such as housecleaning, tending to the queen, making wax, comb construction and repair, sealing cracks, guard duty, ventilating the hive, scouting, foraging and making honey. Bees perform all of these activities for the sake of others in colony and generations to come. But none of these activities could occur if it were not for the bees properly caring for and maintaining a warm environment to develop the next generation of bees.

Regardless of what people think when they see a church—a social gathering, a collection of hypocrites, a learning center for doctrine or a place to meet a spouse—a church should be an incubator for believers of all ages. Any good church will be one that spreads the seeds of the gospel, is patient with those who hear the gospel, nurtures those who are receptive, equips them to be faithful followers of Christ and then sends them out into the world. These believers in turn should spread the gospel message while nurturing and equipping others so that the cycle can continue. A healthy church should be like a pipeline. It is a place where seekers enter at one end and mature committed believers emerge from the other end. Between these two ends there should be people and programs which contribute to the process of building and encouraging all believers to reach maturity.

Many churches are good at being "seeker friendly" as they have little trouble bringing nonbelievers into their midst. They are also good at effectively communicating the essence of the gospel in a clear and pertinent manner. For those that are receptive to the grace of God, the next phase is a lifetime of spiritual growth. How will this occur? Apart from the mysterious working of God's Spirit within the heart, nothing will occur. But believers are all part of the body of Christ, and, as indicated in 1 Corinthians 12, they need one another. They can help one another as the Spirit works through each member of the body.

In 1 Corinthians 12 Paul describes unity amidst diversity. There are different spiritual gifts and offices within the church but the same Source who sovereignly directs the individual members with their unique gifts (v. 18). God's overall purpose for this orchestration of variously gifted individuals is the building up of the body (Ephesians 4:12). Observe what Eugene Peterson writes regarding this passage of Ephesians that beautifully describes spiritual growth occurring among believers to fulfill God's plan within His church.

> He handed out gifts of apostle, prophet, evangelist, and pastor-teacher to train Christians in skilled servant work, working within Christ's body, the church, until we're all moving rhythmically and easily with each other, efficient and graceful in response to God's Son, fully mature adults, fully developed within and without, fully alive like Christ. No prolonged infancies among us, please. We'll not tolerate babes in the woods, small children who are an easy mark for imposters. God wants us to grow up, to know the whole truth and tell it in love—like Christ in everything. We take our lead from Christ, who is the source of everything we do. He keeps us in step with each other. His very breath and blood flow through us, nourishing us so that we will grow up healthy in God, robust in love (*The Message*).

Another scriptural basis for the members of Christ's church to function within mutually beneficial relationships is the "one another" commands in the New Testament. In case these are new to you, or perhaps you have forgotten them, here are most of them:

Love *one another*, even as I (Jesus) have loved you (John 13:34).

Be devoted to *one another* in brotherly love (Romans 12:10).

Give preference to *one another* in honor (Romans 12:10).

Be of the same mind toward *one another* (Romans 12:16).

Building up of *one another* (Romans 14:19).

Accept *one another* (Romans 15:7).

Have the same care for *one another* (1 Corinthians 12:25).

Through love serve *one another* (Galatians 5:13).

Showing tolerance for *one another* in love (Ephesians 4:2).

Be kind to *one another*, tender-hearted, forgiving each other (Ephesians 4:32).

Speaking to *one another* in psalms and hymns (Ephesians 5:19).

Be subject to *one another* in the fear of Christ (Ephesians 5:21).

Regard *one another* as more important than yourselves (Philippians 2:3).

Bearing with *one another*, and forgiving each other (Colossians 3:13).

Teaching and admonishing *one another* (Colossians 3:16).

Increase and abound in love for *one another* (1 Thessalonians 3:12).

Comfort *one another* (1 Thessalonians 4:18).

Encourage *one another* and build up *one another* (1 Thessalonians 5:11).

Live in peace with *one another* (1 Thessalonians 5:13).

Always seek after that which is good for *one another* (1 Thessalonians 5:15).

Stimulate *one another* to love and good deeds (Hebrews 10:24).

Confess your sins to *one another*, and pray for *one another* (James 5:16).

Be hospitable to *one another* (1 Peter 4:9).

Serving *one another* (1 Peter 4:10).

Clothe yourselves with humility toward *one another* (1 Peter 5:5).

We should *love one* another (1 John 3:11).

Throughout almost the entire New Testament—from Jesus' words in the Gospels to John's small epistles—one can see the "one another" commands. Also in the New Testament are "one another" commands stated in the negative (judging, quarreling, challenging, envying and lying to one another) that are to be avoided. Of course, each of these commands needs to be understood within its proper context. But the point is clear that Christians are to function within a community for each other's benefit. So just like a beehive a church should be an incubator where all believers—new and mature alike—can develop in a warm, loving and nurturing environment.

Let's step back for a moment. Few will disagree that Christians should be involved in serving their fellow believers. In fact, many are eager for opportunities to serve. But implied in these commands are two groups of people—the doers and the receivers. In order for "one anothering" to take place, both groups need to exist. Unfortunately many times too few are willing to be recipients. Therefore, those who are willing and able to help others are not used. We all need to lay aside our pride and recognize we can always benefit in some way from those around us. We all just need to lower our guard and allow ourselves to be transparent. When people are real with each other, meaningful interactions and relationships can occur.

Churches that promote small group ministries (house churches, growth groups, cell groups, Bible studies and the like) will repeatedly encourage folks to get to know each other and be willing to be vulnerable and share honestly (but appropriate to the setting) what is going on in their lives. That means sharing the joys and victories as well as the pains and struggles. When group members are genuine with each other bonding will occur, and this is what will make the experience meaningful for everyone. In this open and honest environment real growth can occur as burdens are shared and comfort is gained by knowing you are not alone in the trials of life. But this kind of openness is rare.

"One anothering" can occur spontaneously in one-on-one encounters. It need not be confined to a group. Christian co-workers can enjoy fellowship in the workplace. Friends can chat and share life over a cup of coffee. The ballpark, shopping mall and school are all places where Christians can minister to each other. Jesus said, "For where two or three have gathered together in My name, I am there in their midst" (Matthew 18:20). What a comfort and encouragement to know Jesus will be there to help us when we fellowship with and minister to other believers.

One of the obstacles to meaningful small groups, especially among some believers, is the reluctance to deviate from the traditional knowledge-based teaching or Bible study format. Knowledge is good. Biblical knowledge is great. Putting biblical knowledge into practice in real life is difficult, but it should be the ultimate goal of our learning. What better place to put learning and application together than in a small group of fellow believers who are committed to each other? But it is "safer" just to learn the Scriptures. Some may say they really do not know what the Bible says or find it difficult to understand. Although this may be true for some people, it can be a convenient excuse for not getting involved in the sometimes messy process of "one anothering."

As a seminary graduate I can testify there is literally no end to what one can learn about the Bible. In fact, I almost quit about midway through my program because I felt so inadequate in what I thought I should know in light of how much there was to know. But without knowing my state of discouragement a wise professor offhandedly remarked one evening during a lecture that "the only thing seminary teaches you is how little you know."[5] I took his remark as he intended it—we will be Bible students the rest of our lives. Learning will be an ongoing process but should not interfere with applying the truths of Scripture. We learn and live these truths with one another.

For those who refuse to let go of the traditional Bible study format it should be noted your quest for knowledge of the Scriptures is certainly commendable. Be careful because you may only be feeding your mind. The heart must be engaged in a believer's life in order for real growth to occur. Proverbs 4:23 says, "Watch over your heart with all diligence, for from it flow the springs of life." *The Message* puts it this way: "Keep vigilant watch over your heart; that's where life starts." An honest and caring environment with committed Christian friends is one of the best ways to help keep watch over your heart. We all need people in our lives to know when to ask us the tough probing questions and when to offer us a tender word of encouragement. No amount of head knowledge can teach anyone the art of delivering the right words at the right time. It comes from the heart.

Let me encourage you to trust the leading of God's Spirit in your life regarding your intimate and necessary involvement in the lives of fellow believers. Spiritual growth can be awkward and painful, but it will be worth the effort. It is very congested inside a beehive as thousands of bees move about constantly bumping into one another. But it is this very same congestion that provides the necessary warmth for the developing brood. Let the warm and loving environment of a group of committed Christian friends incubate your heart.

Chapter 5

Cleaning House

By their nature honeybees are very clean creatures. The fervor with which they clean their hive could be a case study of obsessive-compulsive disorder behavior. It starts at a very young age for the bees. It is believed that a newly emerged bee will clean the cell from which it came so the cell is ready for immediate reuse as a crib for another bee or for food storage. Bees will remove any foreign objects or debris that may enter the hive. Interestingly enough there is a sub-category of house cleaners called "undertaker bees" that remove their dead siblings from the hive. Instead of simply dropping the deceased brother or sister to the ground near the hive entrance, an undertaker bee will muster all its strength and airlift the corpse and deposit it a safe distance from the hive to help prevent the start or spread of disease. This fixation with cleanliness is both beneficial for the bees and entertaining for beekeepers.

There are articles describing how beekeepers will place small objects, such as a blade of grass, in the top of the hive as they are finishing their inspection. After closing the top of the hive they will then wait to see how long it takes for the bees to bring the grass to the hive entrance, carry it to the edge of the landing area and then drop it to the ground. A friend once told me that nearly every time he would get into his hive bumblebees would hover around him. Out of irritation he swung at and knocked down one of the bumblebees. Being somewhat sadistic, he carefully picked up the stunned bumblebee and placed it on top of the highest super and sealed its fate by installing the top cover over it. There was no way out for the bumblebee except to go down through the entire hive amidst fifty thousand angry bees.

My friend then waited to see how long it took for his bees to escort the now dead bumblebee down to the entrance and throw it to the ground. It took several minutes, but his wait was rewarded. My friend began to see *pieces* of the bumblebee being carried out from the entrance and unceremoniously tossed overboard. Evidently the bumblebee was too large to fit through the narrow passages of the hive. To solve the problem, the bees dismembered their large guest. Sometimes drastic measures are necessary.

Obviously, the fastidiousness of the bees works greatly to their benefit. Not only do they keep the hive free of large foreign objects that are seen, but the bees also ward off microscopic threats that cannot be seen. Propolis (also called bee glue) is gathered by the bees from certain nearby plants and is spread over the interior of the hive. Propolis has antibiotic properties that protect the hive against bacteria.[1]

Also, when the bees store pollen for consumption during the winter, they mix in some honey with it as well. This honey-pollen mixture interacts with some helpful bacteria that produce lactic acid, a preservative, to protect the pollen. Also, honey by virtue of its own composition will generate a small amount of hydrogen peroxide that is a disinfectant.[2] Thus, these properties of propolis and honey, coupled with a thorough housecleaning, make the beehive an extremely sanitary place.

Bees are not the only creatures that should practice cleanliness. Generally most people like a clean living environment. Of course, liking a clean environment and maintaining one are two different stories. But, given a choice, most people would agree that having a clean home is preferable. Having a clean environment is one thing, but being clean as a person on the inside is also another story. Christians should be as diligent as the bees to practice personal "housecleaning."

Start with the heart. Proverbs 4:23 says, "Watch over your heart with all diligence, for from it flow the springs of life." Along a back country road amidst steep hills was a refreshing stream of water that gently cascaded down the bank along the side of the road. Being tired of city water, people would drive for miles bringing their empty jugs to collect this fresh water. One day, after forming a cup with his hands and drinking this water, a man said, "I wonder where this water comes from?" He then started an uphill climb to follow the stream back to its source through the forest. A few minutes into the hike, the man gagged when he saw the rotting carcass of a dead animal lying in the very stream from which he had just drunk.

Obviously, things are not always as they appear to be. On the outside we may appear to "have it all together." But on the inside we may be hiding things from others as well as ourselves. We need to make sure our hearts are right before the Lord. He knows what is going on in our hearts anyway. "But wait until the Lord comes who will both bring to light the things hidden in the darkness *and disclose the motives of men's hearts*; and then each man's praise will come to him from God" (1 Corinthians 4:5).

The heart is the core of our being. It is where the truest you exists. The things we value have a prominent place in our hearts. Sometimes worthy items are there. Other times there are not. Your heart can be where the Lord Jesus resides. It can also be the place where pride, selfishness, hatred and lust abide.

After a series of sins associated with his affair with Bathsheba, King David, in perhaps the most sincere prayer of the Bible, prayed "Create in me a clean heart, O God, and renew a steadfast spirit within me" (Psalm 51:10). Later in the Psalms King David wrote, "Search me, O God, and know my heart; try me and know my anxious thoughts; and see if there be any hurtful way in me, and lead me in the everlasting way" (Psalm 139:23-24). We all should ask God to search us and reveal hidden sins that may lurk in the dark recesses of our heart.

The mind is the link between the heart and how you live your life. Therefore it is important to have a clean mind. Paul spoke of the mind and how we are to control it. He said that "we are taking every thought captive to the obedience of Christ" (2 Corinthians 10:5) and "set your mind on the things above, not on the things that are on earth" (Colossians 3:2). Taking our thoughts into captivity means to subjugate any way of thinking that is false or contrary to Christ, just as a winning army would subjugate its prisoners of war.[3] Setting our minds on heavenly things simply means to think with an eternal perspective and to realize this world, with all of its trappings, is temporal and perishing.

Our minds are extremely active and wander quickly from subject to subject. This wandering may be spontaneous, or it may be caused by some external stimulus. Therefore ungodly thoughts may enter our minds. The key is not to dwell on them. A person cannot help it if a bird flies overhead, but he can certainly prevent it from building a nest in his hair. The best way to block these negative thoughts is to go on the offensive and fill your mind with healthy things. Paul said it best: "Finally, brethren, whatever is true, whatever is honorable, whatever is right, whatever is pure, whatever is lovely, whatever is of good repute, if there is any excellence and if anything worthy of praise, dwell on these things" (Philippians 4:8). This is an excellent verse to commit to memory and to use in meditation.

When you are relaxing, where do your thoughts go? It may take some effort to police your own thoughts. It is difficult to say whether our thought patterns come from our heart attitudes or whether our ungodly thoughts poison our heart or if both occur. Regardless, try to monitor your thoughts. God will hold you accountable for what you process between your ears.

Acknowledge your shortcomings and sins and ask Him for His forgiveness. "For You, Lord, are good, and ready to forgive, and abundant in loving kindness to all who call upon You" (Psalm 86:5). The Hebrew word for "loving kindness," *hesed*, is used about 250 times in the Old Testament. It refers to the loyal love of a patient, forbearing God toward His people despite their indifference or rebellion. *Hesed* is God's deliberate effort of pursuing His people for the purpose of restoration, forgiveness and fellowship.[4] What a wonderful God we have! He loves us and is committed to us in spite of all our failures—the obvious ones as well as the hidden ones. We need only to respond to Him. Turn over the dark corners of your heart and mind to Him so that Jesus can live through you in those areas.

Finally, we may need to clean up our environment. That does not mean we all need to become conservationists and join the Green Party. It does mean we need to be aware of how our personal surroundings may influence us. The New Testament gives numerous warnings about our surroundings. Some are general while others are specific.

Abstain from every form of evil (1 Thessalonians 5:22).

For the love of money is a root of all sorts of evil, and some by longing for it have wandered away from the faith and pierced themselves with many griefs. But *flee* from these things, you man of God (1 Timothy 6:10-11).

Now *flee* from youthful lusts and pursue righteousness (2 Timothy 2:22).

Beloved, *do not imitate* what is evil, but what is good (3 John 11).

Do not be deceived: "Bad company corrupts good morals" (1 Corinthians 15:33).

In the first four verses above, the italicized verbs are in the imperative mood in the original Greek. They are commands, not suggestions. Commands can be obeyed or not. Delayed obedience is disobedience. In the fifth verse Paul is quoting a Greek proverb from the comic playwright Menander that advised individuals to be mindful of the company they keep.[5]

Now these verses do not mean we are to join a monastery in some desolate location and assume an austere lifestyle to isolate and insulate ourselves from the world's system and all its enticements. These verses mean that although we live in a corrupt world we are not to partake of, or be influenced by, the things that are contrary to Christ and His kingdom. In fact, believers are to be advancing Christ's kingdom in this world.

We need to evaluate our environment carefully. Is it influencing us, or are we influencing it? If someone struggles with certain repetitive or besetting sins, avoid the near occasion of sin. In other words try to avoid situations that cause you to stumble. Such situations may include magazine racks, TV shows, internet sites, certain social settings, casinos or even certain individuals. Sometimes stern measures may be necessary to distance ourselves from situations that cause us to stumble.

Jesus makes a drastic statement about distancing ourselves from sin in the Sermon on the Mount. He said, "If your right eye makes you stumble, tear it out and throw it from you; for it is better for you to lose one of the parts of your body, than for your whole body to be thrown into hell. If your right hand makes you stumble, cut it off and throw it from you; for it is better for you to lose one of the parts of your body, than for your whole body to go into hell" (Matthew 5:29-30). Jesus was speaking here in hyperbole—an exaggeration used to emphasize a point. Jesus' point was that we should apply deadly seriousness to cut out of our lives anything that makes us stumble. Just as the bees dismembered the bumblebee for the sake of the hive so should Christians seek to sever themselves from things that make them compromise their convictions. The key is to know one's own weak areas and then act accordingly.

Housecleaning is hard work whether it is done by honeybees or individuals. One bee could not possibly keep the entire hive clean. She needs the help of thousands of others. We too need the help of our brothers and sisters in Christ. We need close committed relationships with people who care about us and are likewise seeking help and encouragement themselves as they travel along their Christian journey. We need others for several reasons.

One, we need to know we are not alone. It is amazing how many times someone will share a thought or problem, thinking it is unique to them, only to find others firmly nodding their heads in full agreement and understanding. Two, we need objective insight. We do not see ourselves as clearly as we should. Sometimes we think we are "legends in our own minds" or we may be entirely too critical of ourselves. Others can easily provide a balanced assessment of our condition. We all have our own blind spots to our behavior or attitudes that are clearly visible to others. We need the insights of others, and we just simply need to ask. Third, we need to be held accountable and supported by prayer. If left to ourselves, being creatures of habit, we probably will not do what is necessary to address problems. The inquiries of concerned friends, coupled with the knowledge of their faithful prayers, should prompt us and help us to be diligent to keep our personal house clean.

Cleaning the hive of visible and invisible threats minimizes the chance of disease to both the brood and the adult bees alike. Cleanliness helps maintain social order for the bee colony, and it keeps their food supply pure. In short, maintaining a clean hive is essential to the well-being of the colony. Keeping the hive clean is an on-going job for every member of the colony.

Personal housecleaning for Christians is necessary. There are invisible and visible issues to address. One must monitor his or her heart and mind as well as be aware of external things and situations that create problems. Keeping one's heart, mind and life on the right track will always be an ongoing process. Remember that we are not alone. Ask for help.

Chapter 6

Center of Attention

In the beehive the queen bee is by far the single most important member of the colony. She is an egg-laying machine. Estimates of her egg-laying capacity range from one thousand to two thousand eggs per day during the height of the season. The more eggs laid, the more bees there will be. More bees mean a larger work force. The larger the work force, the more chores that can be performed. This means more workers are available to tend to more eggs and developing brood than in the previous generation. If more eggs and brood can be tended, this means the queen can lay eggs at an even greater rate. Thus, a successful upward spiral of productivity can occur in a hive. From a beekeeper's perspective the crowning result of this growth is that more honey can be harvested. Regardless of the perspective of the bees or the beekeepers, success starts with a healthy, active and productive queen.

Although the worker bees are females, the queen is the only fully developed female capable of mating. Being an egg-laying machine, one might be tempted to call her the hive mom. This would be a bit of an exaggeration. Although she does lay eggs, her one and only act of motherhood for her offspring is when she deposits the egg in its cell. She then moves along to the next cell to deposit another egg. Thus she continues without ever looking back. When the eggs hatch, the larvae are fed and cared for by the worker bees.

When discussing honeybee reproduction, several odd, or interesting, items are worthy of note. First, the queen can lay fertilized or unfertilized eggs. She stores in her body the sperm she acquired during her mating flights from her various suitors. Thus, within her body she can control which eggs will become fertilized and which will not. Worker bees develop from fertilized eggs whereas drones come from unfertilized eggs. In other words, the workers have a father, but the drones do not. Another interesting quirk in bee breeding is that the workers possess features not present in either of their parents. For example, neither the queen nor the drones have pollen baskets on their back legs, and yet the worker bees do. Also, the worker bee has a barbed stinger while the drones have no stinger at all, and the queen has a basically straight stinger. Some other traits possessed by the offspring but not present in the parents include certain glands and a longer tongue.

Now back to the queen. A queen bee develops from a fertilized egg just as a worker bee does. But queen larva is fed a special substance called royal jelly throughout its entire growth which will cause it to develop into a queen. Worker larvae are fed royal jelly but only for a short duration of their development. Thus, it is the difference in a larva's diet that determines if she will be a worker or a queen.[1] It is the worker bees who feed the larvae and who decide if the colony needs a new queen. New queens are needed when a swarm is being planned, when the existing queen is weak and doing a poor job, or if the queen dies. Once the decision is made, worker bees will select several newly laid eggs to develop into queens. The larvae from these eggs are only fed the royal jelly.

If a beekeeper determines he wants to start a new colony, he basically has two choices. He can order a colony with a queen bee from a commercial apiary, or he can "divide" an existing colony. If he chooses the latter, he will begin by withdrawing a few frames of brood from an existing hive. He needs to be sure newly laid eggs are on these frames. He will also have to ensure he does not accidentally remove the queen bee from the existing hive during this process. The frames with the eggs and the brood are placed into a new super that will be their new home when they emerge as adult bees. The beekeeper must also take some worker bees from the existing hive to tend to the brood. He will close off the entrance of the new home so that the worker bees and brood are confined for about a day. During this period of confinement the worker bees will sense the absence of a queen. Within a few hours of sensing the absence of a queen, they will choose some of the eggs on the frames to develop into queens.[2] When the hive entrance is opened, it is hoped these workers will carry on as they did in their original hive and perform their duties in their new home and go out and gather food for the upstart colony.

Queen cells are easy to identify. Because queens are longer than a worker or a drone, their cells are noticeably longer. The exterior of queen cells will be raised and have a dimpled texture similar to that of a peanut shell. If all goes well, at least one queen will emerge in sixteen days. Once she emerges from her cell, the new queen will go around the hive and kill the other queens before they hatch. She does this by thrusting her stinger through the wax cell, thus fatally impaling the queen inside. If two queens emerge at the same time, they will usually fight to the death and the winner will be the new queen of the hive.

The new queen will hang around inside the hive for a few days before venturing out on her mating flights. She does not go on her mating flight immediately after hatching because her body is still developing. Once ready, she takes off. She is a strong flier and only the fastest and healthiest of the drones will be able to catch her to mate with her in the air. The future of the hive depends upon her successfully mating and safely returning to the hive. Her success is crucial because at this point in time no new eggs are in the hive from which to develop another queen.

Upon returning to the hive, the new queen must begin laying eggs as quickly as possible. It will take twenty-one days for the first eggs to hatch, develop and emerge as desperately needed replacement workers. Since the population of this newly started hive was already low and bees live only several weeks anyway, any delay in laying eggs could do irreparable damage to this fledgling colony's hope of survival. If too many of the workers from the original hive die before being replaced, there may not be enough bees to properly warm and tend to the developing brood. If the brood does not develop and dies, the colony will then be in a fatal downward spiral. So the key to the success of starting a new hive is dependent upon the worker bees raising a new queen and her ability to start laying eggs as soon as possible. When compared to other hives, if a beekeeper notices idle bees at the entrance and no bees are bringing in any pollen, then he has reason to believe there is a problem with the queen.[3]

Just as the survival of a new hive hinges upon the performance of a queen bee, the same is true of an existing hive. A strong worker force is needed to gather and store food for the coming winter, let alone gather food for the existing colony members and developing brood. To have a strong work force, the queen must do her job and do it well. A good queen will lay her eggs in a solid pattern in the center area of the frame. (The edges of the frame are filled with honey and pollen. Thus, these supplies are readily available to feed to the developing brood by the nurse bees.) A scattered brood pattern is a sign of a poorly performing queen. If the queen is not performing well, the beekeeper may introduce a new queen into the hive to correct the situation. The bees themselves may replace a poorly performing queen by developing a new queen as was described above. When the bees replace their queen it is called "superceding." This new queen will have to venture out on a mating flight and return safely prior to picking up where her mother left off before she was unceremoniously dismissed from the hive.

Sometimes beekeepers may want to change the ill-tempered mood of the bees in a particular hive. To change its temperament, the beekeeper will take action to re-queen the hive. A new queen's offspring will have different characteristics from those of the old queen and thus will change the overall temperament of the colony. To replace a queen, the beekeeper will go into a hive, find her, remove her and insert a queen from a commercial supplier. This new queen will come in a little box with screened sides and a small entrance that is plugged with candy. When the old queen is removed, the box with the new queen is placed inside the hive. Initially the bees recognize her as a stranger and are hostile to her. But as the scent of the old queen fades and the scent of the new queen replaces it the bees start to accept her. Meanwhile, the bees will eat through the candy door to release her. The time it takes for them to eat through the door allows her scent to spread through the hive and thus improves the chances she will be accepted by the colony.

Sometimes when replacing a queen the beekeeper will simply remove the old queen and allow the bees to make a new queen as in the process described above when they develop a new queen from a freshly laid egg. Although this is a less expensive method of replacing a queen, it is not the optimal method. Without a queen no eggs are being laid to replenish the population. Since it will be several weeks before a new queen can be raised and mated and start laying eggs, the population of the colony will decrease until the new queen's offspring emerge. Therefore, to minimize the disruption caused by replacing a queen, it is better to introduce a new queen that has already been bred and is ready to get to work once she is released from her box.

After a queen bee has mated she will return to the hive and begin her "reign." She is actually more of a figurehead than a ruler. It is believed "control bees"[4] may be calling the shots. These control bees are believed to be a small group of workers that determine such things as if and when the colony will swarm or if a new queen is needed to replace the current one. If there are control bees in charge, then the queen is simply a reproduction specialist and is basically just another worker bee with a unique job. If there is no such thing as control bees, then the hive activities are directed by instinct as the bees respond to various conditions and by chemical emissions called pheromones.

One thing the queen does is emit pheromones. If nothing else, her pheromones help maintain social order in the hive and give its members a unique identity or scent. This scent helps the guard bees to know who belongs in the hive and who does not. The role of pheromones in a hive is only barely understood, and their chemical compositions are even more elusive. The bees, however, seem to have no problem deciphering the coded messages of the pheromones as seen in their methodical and efficient society.

As the queen goes about her business of laying eggs, she is continually surrounded by her own personal entourage. These attendants feed, groom and dispose of her "business." Sometimes beekeepers can find the queen by first spotting this small group of attendants clustered together around her. Because her attendants are constantly interacting with her, they receive her scent or pheromones. As these attendants interact with other bees within the hive, the pheromones are eventually passed on to every member of the colony.[5] Thus, the colony gets a regular dose of the pheromone to maintain its unique identifier.

In summary, the queen is the single most important member of the hive and is the center of attention of the colony. Although she can be replaced, the period of transition to a new queen is a vulnerable time for the colony whether it is new or already well established. As the queen performs, so will the entire colony. If she does poorly, the colony suffers due to a reduced workforce. If she does her job well, the colony will prosper because a large workforce can sustain itself and also harvest and store a surplus of food that is necessary for future colony members to survive the winter. The pheromones of the queen help keep order and provide a unique form of identification for the colony. Without a queen or the ability to make one a colony is doomed regardless of its size.

In almost any church today, the central figure is the pastor or priest. Whether a church is large or small, it typically cannot survive without a pastor. Some pastors call the shots in their church. At some churches the pastor shares leadership responsibilities with other individuals. In still other churches the pastor is under the direction of a board. Regardless of the pastor's place in leadership, he plays a crucial role in the life of the church.

Pastors' roles will vary from church to church depending upon the situation. In a newly planted church the pastor must be a special individual in order to deal with the unique demands of this situation. As the initial excitement of starting a new church fades, he must lead the charge and rally the troops as the first few years will probably have more "downs" than "ups." Attendance will probably shrink from the initial meeting as well-wishers return to their home churches and those looking for specific attributes or ministries (usually associated with larger churches) will move on. The pastor will also have to do a lot of the "grunt" work such as setting up and tearing down a rented facility for Sunday services. Starting a new church is not for the faint of heart.

In small, established churches the pastor can usually shed some of the behind-the-scenes work as others will volunteer to help. But in this type of church the pastor still has to wear multiple hats. He will oversee the youth group. He will provide counsel for the various needs that will arise such as helping those who are deciding to get married or those whose marriages are about to fail. He will console those grieving the loss of a loved one. He will perform hospital and hospice visitations. He will be the "go-to" guy for everyone's spiritual and theological questions. In other words, this pastor is a very busy individual. If the church grows, it is hoped the pastor's strategy for ministry will adapt. If he tries to be the "go-to" guy for a church with two hundred or more members as he did when the church had only one hundred members, either he will fail or the church members will suffer. It will only be a matter of time.

In larger churches there is usually a pastoral staff and a division of labor among the various pastors as they each lead different ministries. The number of pastors is usually reflective of the size of the congregation. With a good staff these churches continue to grow numerically as they feed upon their own success. The variety of pastors under the same steeple will usually provide a good mix of approaches and personalities. This smorgasbord of ministers usually allows individuals within the congregation to find at least one pastor with whom they can connect, and thus they will remain at the church.

Regardless of its size or development the church will usually take on the characteristics or passions of the pastor or pastors. Most churches now have mission statements that were probably developed completely or at least with input from the pastor. If the pastor has a heart for overseas missions, so will the church. If the pastor emphasizes small groups, then the church will strive to have a small group ministry. If the pastor emphasizes social issues so will the church. Whatever the pastor's passion may be, so also will be the primary passion of the church. Thus, pastors usually provide a sense of identity or purpose for their congregations. If their plans or passions meet with opposition, then that pastor's time at that church will probably be limited and a replacement will be sought.

Power struggles within a church should not happen, but unfortunately they do. Whenever frail and flawed people are involved (and Christians certainly are no exception), problems will arise. We all have egos that to some extent will get in the way and create conflict. The best any group of believers can hope to achieve in running a church is to have leaders who are humble and dependent upon God's leading. When problems arise (and they will), it is hoped the opposing parties will quickly strive to correct the impasse in a spirit of love, unity and peace (Ephesians 4:1-3). If a change of pastors is necessary, the church members should not be as cold and calculating as the bees when they replace a struggling queen bee. Honesty and communications will be the keys in arriving at a mutually beneficial solution for all parties involved.

Aside from leadership responsibilities and providing a vision or identity for a church, pastors are primarily known for their teaching. If they can connect with their congregation, then they will usually be successful. If they are unable to teach in a manner that resonates with their flock, then something is going to change. Either the pastor will have to try to change his approach (it may be difficult, though, to change style or forsake a passion); the congregation will vote with their feet and move on to another church; or the congregation will vote for another pastor. The teaching will make all the difference in the life of a church. Either the pastor can do it, or he cannot. The congregation, however, is not completely absolved of responsibility. It can either respond to the teaching or not. So if there is "a problem with the pastor" it should be determined who is having the problem—the pastor or the congregation.

The pastor's teaching can be likened to spreading seeds. The seeds of truth must be sown in the hearts and minds of the congregation and the surrounding community. Who else has such a regular platform from which to influence others? Being a pastor with this kind of influence is an awesome responsibility and needs to be taken quite seriously. James wrote, "Let not many of you become teachers, my brethren, knowing that as such we will incur a stricter judgment" (James 3:1). One of my seminary professors, in referring to this verse, stated in a serious tone that he had a tremendous responsibility to teach the Scriptures accurately to his students. Knowing he was speaking to a room full of potential pastors, he said that if he made an error in his teaching it would be like a virus that could spread rapidly through the teaching of his students and continue for generations.[6]

Another great responsibility of pastors is to love God as they tend to their flock. In John 21, Jesus repeatedly asked Peter if he loved Him. Following each of Peter's responses, Jesus said to the effect, "Take care of My sheep." It is interesting for pastors and priests to note the connection between the greatest commandment (to love God) and that of tending to the care of the congregation. It would also bode well for pastors to remember John 21 states that Jesus is the owner of the sheep not the pastors.

Tending the flock should be at the core of every pastor's ministry. Caring for his congregation can occur in countless forms and take place in various locales. Just as the queen provides her colony with a unique identity, so also pastors can provide their own unique influence or passion to their churches. If a queen bee does not do an adequate job in her primary role as egg layer, the colony will be threatened. If a pastor is negligent in his roles, the church will also be threatened. Being the center of attention, whether in a beehive or in a church, is an awesome responsibility. It is hoped pastors will be like the queen bees that are surrounded by dedicated and caring supporters who will help them fulfill their roles.

Chapter 7

Drones

The drones are the males within the honeybee society. They can only be found within a hive during the warm months. Typically there may be anywhere between several hundred to a few thousand drones in a hive. Therefore they account for only a relatively small percentage of the overall population of a colony. What determines the drone population? The answers are uncertain and vary, but it probably has to do with the health of the queen, the overall health of the colony or if a swarm is about to take place. The queen can choose to lay an egg that will develop into a worker bee or a drone based upon the size of the cell. Since drones are bigger than worker bees, they need a larger cell in which to develop. The worker bees that make the cells somehow know when and how many drone-sized cells to make.

Drones live only about a month. This seems to be an unusually short lifespan. Worker bees, their sisters, typically live a few weeks longer. The short life of the worker bees is attributable to the fact that they work themselves to death. Drones, on the other hand, do no work whatsoever. They do not even have a stinger to defend the hive or themselves for that matter. Regardless of how long they live, drones do have two passions in life—mating and eating. (Some things remain the same throughout the animal kingdom.) Perhaps their short lifespan is because they die of frustration or are bored to death because of their lazy lifestyle.

Regarding their first passion, it should be understood that mating takes place in flight. A queen bee will only mate during an early phase of her life. When she leaves the hive to mate, she will fly to what scientists call a "drone congregation area"[1] or what some beekeepers call a "drone zone." A drone zone is an area where drones fly around and wait for a queen to show up. When the queen arrives in the area, a chase begins. (Strangely enough, the drones seem to ignore a queen when they are together within the hive.[2]) Typically the queen will be a little faster than the drones. The drone who catches her will be the one to mate with her. This chasing process weeds out the slower and weaker drones so that only the best and healthiest drone will mate and thus pass on his good traits ensuring a strong species. Given the competition and the rarity of finding a queen, a drone is extremely lucky if he gets to mate. But at the same time he is extremely unlucky. As a result of mating, the drone will die[3] but will do so with a little smile on his face.

As far as their second passion goes, females are involved as well. Drones must be fed by the worker bees. The drones do not have the ability to forage for food outside of the hive, nor do they feed themselves from the stored honey within the hive. Worker bees must stop what they are doing to feed a drone when he is hungry. This seems to be the height of laziness. Given the fact that the drones make no contribution to the colony, it seems extremely unfair and inefficient that they are spoiled by the workforce. Surprisingly some studies seem to indicate that colonies with more drones produce more honey than those with less.[4] For the drones, however, all good things come to an end.

To improve its chances of surviving the winter, the colony will conserve its precious food supply by reducing the number of mouths to feed. In the fall, usually after the first frost, as the colony is making final preparations for winter, the drones are left out in the cold—literally. One day life is fine for the lazy drones. The next day the workers turn upon their brothers. It is believed that the workers' initial act of betrayal involves withholding food from the drones. Being weakened from a lack of food, the drones are then battered and harassed by their smaller sisters. The drones that get the message will flee the hive but will not be permitted to re-enter. Those drones that stay and hope for the return of the good old days are unceremoniously dragged out of the hive. For those drones that stubbornly refuse to accept their fate and insist on re-entering their home, they will find themselves being impaled with a stinger.

The drones are useless to the colony aside from the "lucky" few who donate their DNA for the continuation of the species. When the season of tolerance and generosity is over, these useless creatures meet a harsh fate. In God's kingdom, like in a beehive, there is always work to be done and there will be a day of reckoning. Therefore do not be a drone.

The Book of Proverbs contains many warnings about being lazy while also extolling the virtues of diligence. Although there are no proverbs specifically about bees (or drones), here are two proverbs that are close:

> Go to the ant, O sluggard, observe her ways and be wise, which, having no chief, officer or ruler, prepares her food in the summer and gathers her provision in the harvest. How long will you lie down, O sluggard? When will you arise from your sleep? "A little sleep, a little slumber, a little folding of the hands to rest"—your poverty will come in like a vagabond and your need like an armed man (Proverbs 6:6-11).

> As the door turns on its hinges, so does the sluggard on his bed. The sluggard buries his hand in the dish; he is weary of bringing it to his mouth again (Proverbs 26:14-15).

In the New Testament, Jesus tells a parable of a man who went on a journey. But before he left he entrusted pieces of silver to three of his slaves. One received five, the second received two, and the third received one. Each one was given an amount according to his own ability. The parable says that the first two doubled their allotment. The third did nothing with his piece of silver. The first two were praised. But Jesus described the third one as a "wicked, lazy slave" (Matthew 25:26). This parable is not about how much money each slave initially received but instead about their being accountable for what they received. Some use their God-given gifts and resources while others do not.[5]

The Bible teaches that each believer has been given at least one spiritual gift (1 Peter 4:10). These gifts are listed in several different passages (1 Peter 4:10-11; Romans 12:3-8; Ephesians 4:7-13; 1 Corinthians 12:7-10, 28-30). But among these lists are words of admonition stating to the effect that the gifts are to be used for the benefit of others within the church. Determine what gift or gifts God has entrusted to you and seek to use them to help others in their walk of faith. Also be prepared to receive assistance or input from others as they use their gifts.

A specific passage addressing "drones" within the early church is 2 Thessalonians 3:10-15:

> For even when we were with you, we used to give you this order: if anyone is not willing to work, then he is not to eat, either. For we hear that some among you are leading an undisciplined life, doing no work at all, but acting like busybodies. Now such persons we command and exhort in the Lord Jesus Christ to work in quiet fashion and eat their own bread. But as for you, brethren, do not grow weary of doing good. If anyone does not obey our instruction in this letter, take special note of that person

and do not associate with him, so that he will be put to shame. Yet do not regard him as an enemy, but admonish him as a brother.

Paul had to write this paragraph to address those who had a misunderstanding (or overemphasis) regarding Christ's return. Since some believed that Christ would return very soon, they quit working to support themselves. Paul addressed the issue of Christ's return in both of his letters to the Thessalonians. It was, and is, an important topic. Evidently it generated a lot of questions and resulted in confusion, causing Paul to address the issue of idleness in both epistles.[6] From our perspective twenty centuries later it seems ridiculous that people had quit working and were waiting around for Christ's return. Even in recent history there are accounts of those who thought they knew the day when Christ would return. They and their followers would go out on a hillside to wait to be taken to heaven. At the end of the day they were disappointed. Simply waiting around for Christ's return is nothing but selfishness. One would think that if someone truly believed Christ was going to return on a given day they would spend that last day telling others about Him because those left behind would be facing a horrible period of tribulation. To sit around and wait to be whisked off to heaven seems contrary to Jesus' parable of the talents. Why sit around and do nothing?

The drone bees seem to have a pretty good life—while it lasts. Christians, like drones, will have a day of reckoning. The application point for this chapter is simple: get to work. Get involved in the lives of others by being a blessing to them and by letting them bless you. There will always be those who manage to find excuses for not getting involved. However, we all will give an account of our lives (Romans 14:12). Do not let the inactivity of others distract you from doing God's work. Christ will return one day. May He find us busy building His kingdom here on earth using the gifts He has given to us.

Chapter 8

Communications

The combined effort of the members of a honeybee colony is truly amazing when one considers the activities that are occurring. Many of these activities are taking place simultaneously, such as housecleaning, nursery duty and foraging, to name a few. Some activities are performed by a large portion of the colony that drop what they are doing to join a group activity such as swarming, defending the hive or gathering water during a heat emergency. When one considers forty to sixty thousand honeybees can be in a single hive, it is even more amazing everything gets done on cue. As with any successful venture good communications are essential. Within a hive, although the bees do not say a word, effective communications that contribute to the success of the colony are taking place.

Bees can communicate through two basic methods. The first and most prevalent method is through scents called pheromones. Pheromones are different from hormones. Pheromones pass from one individual to another of the same species whereas hormones are internal to a creature. Pheromones are secreted by various members of the hive. The queen can keep order and give the colony members a sense of identity by a pheromone called "queen substance." Her scent also acts as a lure to attract drones during mating. Bee larvae can emit pheromones that basically say "feed me" and thus prompt worker bees to increase their pollen-gathering activities. Guard bees emit an alarm pheromone that will put the rest of the bees in a state of heightened alert. When bees sting someone or some creature they are essentially tagging the victim as a target. The stinger, securely attached, will emit a pheromone that will act as a homing beacon to lead other bees to enemy. There are pheromones left behind by the bees as they walk to identify friendly turf for fellow hive members or to mark the location of a new home for a swarm.[1]

Even dead bees emit a pheromone. This scent puts out a message that says, "Hey, I'm dead. You can drag my sorry carcass out of the hive and dump it somewhere." Scientists have identified and replicated this chemical. They have even applied it to a live bee and have observed other bees trying to drag the marked bee out of the hive thinking it was dead.[2] (Who says scientists don't have any fun?) Scientists have been able to identify and replicate only a few other pheromones. One such substance has been used to attract and capture swarms that would otherwise flee into the wild.[3]

Pheromones are complex chemical compounds that are difficult to identify, let alone replicate. The complexity of pheromone composition is an interesting aside. It is amazing that mankind, with all of his learning and technology, struggles to unravel the mysteries of these pheromones. For those who subscribe to the evolutionary theory it must be somewhat of a dilemma that a supposedly mindless nature could randomly concoct such a complex brew of chemicals that stumps the rational mind of man. In the humble opinion of the author such complexities of nature that outwit mankind are clear evidence of the deliberate work of a Creator. Even if man can eventually unlock all the mysteries surrounding these pheromones, it would still leave the question of how such complexities appeared in the first place and how they came to serve such specific communications functions. Aside from their composition there is also an imperfect understanding of the effects of the already known pheromones. No doubt there are still pheromones yet to be identified. These pheromones relay encrypted messages only decipherable by the bees and God.

The second method of communication by bees is dancing. In light of the sophisticated chemical codes in pheromones simple dance routines almost do not seem to fit into the repertoire of the honeybee. But the dances are a language even humans have been able to interpret. The dances are used by scout bees to communicate information to potential foragers regarding needed supplies such as water, pollen or nectar. The types of dances vary depending upon the distance of the source from the hive. Basically there are round dances for short distances and "wagtail" dances for longer distances. These dances are performed on the vertical surfaces of the frames within the hive.

The round dance, as the name implies, is when the scout bee will move around in a circle. The energy of the dance will communicate the quality of the source. Bees desire to be efficient in their foraging efforts. Therefore, if two bees are dancing in close proximity, the bee with the liveliest dance will get more attention and thus influence more bees to visit her discovered source. The dancing scout bees provide additional information about their finds. They will briefly stop their dance and provide samples of their discoveries to those observing the dance. Also the scout bee will provide an aroma of the targeted flower. Traces of the aroma adhere to the bee's body.[4] As other bees contact the dancing bee, they can "smell" the aroma on the scout bee. Therefore, armed with a taste of the source and the associated aroma, foragers will head out to the field clearly knowing what they are looking for. Round dances do not communicate direction. But because the source is relatively near the hive the foragers will not likely miss it, being armed with the information they have coupled with the fact that bees have a keen sense of smell and can detect flowers up to one mile away.[5]

Wagtail dances are a little more complicated. Characteristics of this dance communicate the direction and the distance at which the source is located. This dance pattern is basically a figure-eight as the bee will make one loop and then make the adjacent one. As with the round dance the liveliness of the dance provides a sense of profitability regarding the source. The dancing bee will also stop to provide samples and let others identify the aroma. The key to the wagtail dance is the orientation of the common side of the adjacent loops. The bees compare the orientation of this common side with a straight-up imaginary vertical line. The angle between the common side and the vertical line provides the bees with a direction relative to the position of the sun. For example, if the dancer makes a figure-eight that is lying on its side, such that the common side of the two loops is oriented straight up and down on the face of the frame, then the source of food is either directly toward the sun or away from it depending upon the direction the dancer moved along this common side.

The distance the source is from the hive is "broadcast" by the dancer as she moves. While dancing, the bee will emit sounds at a certain frequency. Although bees have no ears to hear it is believed they can feel the vibrations of this sound. Studies have indicated a direct relationship exists between the time a scout bee spends making this sound and the distance to the intended location.[6]

Whether the round dance or wagtail dance is performed, the dancing bee will repeat the dance pattern several times. This is necessary because the crowd surrounding the dancer has to physically touch the dancer to obtain the message of the dance. The bees need to know what type of dance is being performed. It is unlikely the observers can see which dance is being performed because of the crowd surrounding the dancer and also because the inside of the hive is almost completely dark. Therefore, to get the full effect of the dance observers will have to observe the dance along multiple locations of the dance pattern.

In summary, honeybees use pheromones and dances to communicate crucial information. With so many members in a hive it is essential that communication takes place because many times their survival is at stake. With so many members it is often necessary to repeat or relay the message many times so all can be properly informed. Church members can learn much in this regard from the bees. Communication is necessary for the healthy operation of a church. Also messages must be repeated in order to ensure everyone is informed and on the same page.

Humans communicate through two basic methods—the written word and the spoken word. The written word has evolved over time from handwritten messages to printed pages and now to electronic form such as e-mail. This method works only proportionately to the skill levels of the writer and reader. Writers today can use computers to check their spelling and grammar before sending a message. Clarity of expression ultimately depends upon the author. But there will always be those who have the unique gift to misinterpret or obfuscate a written message regardless of how well it is crafted.

In an effort to explain miscommunications that occur from written messages, we all know letters and symbols can do only so much. The written medium does not convey the mood, tone, emphasis or body language of the author. In one professional work office one of the managers had to address a minor problem that had occurred because people had misread or taken offense at others' e-mails. The authors were not intending any ill will, but without the nonverbal cues just mentioned the stage was set for misinterpretation to occur when quickly reading a hastily prepared e-mail.

So when today's technology fails in the art of written communications, humans revert to what came first—the spoken word. Speaking does have advantages over writing. For example, it is easier and quicker to communicate with someone face-to-face because the nonverbal cues are readily apparent and there can be instantaneous feedback either verbally or nonverbally. But when we speak we are usually much less formal and precise than we would be if we were writing. For instance I have struggled to describe various aspects of the bees in this book. It would have been much easier if you, the reader, were present with me and I could simply point at something rather than use words to describe it. But because we tend to be rather informal and imprecise when speaking, the hearer may misinterpret or misunderstand what is said. Many times communications cause problems or exacerbate existing ones. When this occurs, then further communication is necessary to resolve the problem.

The Bible provides numerous warnings about potential pitfalls regarding the words we say. The Book of Proverbs addresses the spoken word many times. "When there are many words, transgression is unavoidable, but he who restrains his lips is wise" (10:19). "A gentle answer turns away wrath, but a harsh word stirs up anger" (15:1). "Death and life are in the power of the tongue, and those who love it will eat its fruit" (18:21). Jesus issued a strong warning about the words we speak. "But I tell you that every careless word that people speak, they shall give an accounting for it in the day of judgment. For by your words you will be justified, and by your words you will be condemned" (Matthew 12:36-37).

Of course Paul always has something to say about Christian behavior. "Let no unwholesome word proceed from your mouth, but only such a word as is good for edification according to the need of the moment, so that it will give grace to those who hear" (Ephesians 4:29). "And there must be no filthiness and silly talk, or coarse jesting, which are not fitting, but rather giving of thanks" (Ephesians 5:4). "But now you also, put them all aside: anger, wrath, malice, slander, and abusive speech from your mouth" (Colossians 3:8).

James weighs in on the subject with some good advice. "But everyone must be quick to hear, slow to speak and slow to anger; for the anger of man does not achieve the righteousness of God" (James 1:19-20). "If anyone thinks himself to be religious, and yet does not bridle his tongue but deceives his own heart, this man's religion is worthless" (James 1:26). But perhaps no place in Scripture are the perils of thoughtless words better described than by James. "So also the tongue is a small part of the body, and yet it boasts of great things. See how great a forest is set aflame by such a small fire! And the tongue is a fire, the very world of iniquity; the tongue is set among our members as that which defiles the entire body, and sets on fire the course of our life, and is set on fire by hell. For every species of beasts and birds, of reptiles and creatures of the sea, is tamed and has been tamed by the human race. But no one can tame the tongue; it is a restless evil and full of deadly poison" (James 3:5-8).

It is readily apparent the tongue can be deliberately used in negative and harmful ways. Unfortunately, this does occur within the church. Also, unfortunately, negative and harmful messages occur unintentionally. We all have been irritated by a last-minute change in plans that were not effectively communicated throughout the group. And we all can relate to situations when we were the only ones in the group to be overlooked when information was being disseminated. When these things happen it is easy to be angry or hurt and begin to suspect they were done intentionally. If we let these thoughts fester, they will act as a poison in our relationships with those who failed us.

Being the one who is left out of the communication loop can be a hurtful experience. Being on the other side—the one who forgot to contact everyone—can be no fun either. If you fail to contact someone and that person confronts you about it later, the conversation may not be too pleasant. One time my wife, Brenda, was asked to coordinate a church banquet in celebration of a major milestone. She dutifully made arrangements for the dining location and coordinated all the meal requests. She made sure the place would be properly decorated to make the celebration a special event. She carefully planned to have all the necessary people in place such as the keynote speaker, people to pray and individuals to lead a brief time of worship.

Since the banquet was Saturday evening she had asked some of the backup worship team members to help out with the worship. She did this so the regular worship team, scheduled to be lead worship at church on the following morning, would not have to worry about preparing for both the Saturday evening celebration and Sunday morning worship. Furthermore, another reason for using the backup members was to allow the regular worship team members, who had played a significant part in the life of our young church, a chance to be ministered to during the celebration.

Well, as the saying goes, "No good deed goes unpunished." A few days before the celebration when everything was ready to go, a person from the church called Brenda. This person was somewhat blunt and agitated when speaking to my wife. Why? This person was extremely upset because Brenda had not cleared the use of the backup worship team members with the worship team leader. It was true Brenda did not check with the worship team leader (and in hindsight should have done so). She felt she was acting within the authorization given to her by the pastor to do whatever was necessary to make the banquet a special time for the church. Regardless of my wife's explanations, this individual refused to believe Brenda's intentions were honorable and no disrespect was intended. In hindsight this person's strong reaction was caused largely by an unfulfilled (and unexpressed) expectation that all worship-related activities were to go through the worship team leader. This whole event left Brenda wounded and somewhat disillusioned about the people within the church because some had assumed the worst about her and her motives.

In a church, as with any organization, clear communications are essential. Those who are blessed with the special ability to organize and administrate must not forget to keep everyone informed. Communications can be hard work because it may not be readily apparent who needs to be in the loop. For example, if a church is having a special service or series of meetings, a lot of planning will need to occur. An agenda will be coordinated by the planning committee. Special equipment and props will be identified and obtained. Advertising plans will be developed and implemented. Decorations and food will be brought in and set up. Steps will be taken to ensure that child care will be provided. Musicians will be lined up, and the selected music will be practiced. Notebooks or handouts will be printed and ready to distribute to the attendees. The preparations are almost endless. But when the big day arrives it becomes apparent that someone forgot to include the parking team to ensure there is traffic control in the parking lot. Ooops!

Communicate, communicate, communicate. If one has to err in communications, it should be on the side of over-communicating, not under-communicating. Also, whenever people interact, it is good to remember a lot of grace and forgiveness are needed to get through any conflict whether it is real or perceived. Above all else do not forget love. "Above all, keep fervent in your love for one another, because love covers a multitude of sins" (1 Peter 4:8). The application of love Peter spoke of is used to deal with interpersonal problems that have already occurred. In other words, it is an act of love to forgive someone for an infraction.

But Christians should also be practicing love on the "front end" just as the bees do. If you have ever peered into a healthy hive, you will be absolutely amazed that so many bees can fit into the small spaces between the frames. Imagine being confined in closed quarters with sixty thousand of your closest friends! Inside the hive the bees are constantly bumping into and brushing against one another. They frequently walk over one another. On top of the congestion this friction takes place in almost complete darkness. For the bees they simply accept this as normal and take no offense as they patiently continue on with their individual duties. They realize no harm or maliciousness was intended by their fellow hive-mates. The bees can tolerate this environment because they believe the best about each other. In 1 Corinthians 13:7 the apostle Paul said, "(Love) bears all things, believes all things, hopes all things, endures all things." Many problems within a church could be avoided if the members simply gave the offending person or persons the benefit of the doubt and believed the best in them. Not to do so is to fail to love them. By failing to love them, we are in sin.

Bee Parables

Communicate, communicate, communicate. Bees do it. They have to—their survival and common good are at stake. Identify your audience within the church. Then tell them what you are going to tell. Then tell them what you want to tell them. Finally tell them what you just told them. If you are the recipient of a communication, try to listen closely. Regardless of all our efforts, communication breakdowns will occur. Try to the best of your ability to set things right when they occur. We need to be patient, loving and forgiving with our fellow believers. Remember that Jesus is patient, loving and forgiving with us.

Chapter 9

Personal Business

Healthy bees don't poop in the hive.[1]

One of the reasons the inside of a beehive is almost entirely free of harmful bacteria is that bees take care of their personal "business" in a proper manner. The method the bees use is called a "cleansing flight." When a bee heeds nature's call, it will do so in flight. During the warmer months when the bees are normally flying, they regularly take care of business while traveling to perform other necessary missions, and thus they are multitasking.

But during the winter months things can get backed up. In the winter, although the bees are not nearly as active as during the warmer months, they still eat, and thus their bodies produce waste. But the bees simply do not relieve themselves in an empty cell out of sight when no other bee is watching. Instead they hold it. Bees theoretically cannot fly if the air temperature is lower than about 50° F. When there is a break in the weather and the air is warm enough to their liking, the bees take to the air for a cleansing flight or, from another point of view, a bombing run.

I confess I never gave much thought to bees and their toilet training. But one mild winter's weekend day when I was going out to run a late-morning errand, I noticed a bunch of little yellowish-green spots all over my car. Where did they come from? I was at a loss to explain the spots and could only imagine I had recently been driving behind a truck that was spilling who-knows-what and it had splattered on my car. After I returned from my errand I walked to my backyard to check on my hive. I was surprised at the amount of activity as dozens of bees were coming and going. Then the light came on. My car was parked about one hundred feet directly in front of the hive. The interesting fact was that our garage was directly between the hive and my car. Evidently many of the bees had flown the same flight pattern, over or around the garage, on their cleansing flights to result in so many "hits" on my car. I would have thought their flight patterns would have been more random given the fact they can fly several miles. Apparently, because their payload was so heavy and the air was somewhat cool, they opted for a shorter flight.

By their nature bees do not defecate in the hive. Their mutual respect for each other helps maintain social order. It is only rarely that bees defecate in the hive. Occasionally bees get a disease called *nosema*[2] that affects their stomachs and causes diarrhea. The signs of such a disease are brownish splotches near the entrance of the hive. If the condition is too severe, the colony will die because it has been weakened by the disease, or they abandon the hive due to the mess. The only bee that can poop in the hive is the queen. Since she leaves the hive only to mate or during a swarm she does not participate in cleansing flights. Some poor worker bee follows behind the queen with a pooper-scooper to clean up.

To maintain a proper and healthy environment in our churches we need to take care of business properly. By *business* I do not mean churches need to upgrade their restroom facilities. By *business* I am referring to the way we resolve problems or confront individuals within our churches when the need arises.

Matthew 18 speaks of a process for church discipline. First, a meeting needs to occur with the effected person in a one-on-one encounter. If that does not resolve the issue, then the individual is to be approached by several others. If that still does not work, then the entire church is to be involved. The ultimate purpose of confrontation is to help the individual get back on track. But the direction is clear—initiate this process in a private one-on-one chat. If the individual is not receptive, then the process involves progressively calling in additional help.

Throughout the New Testament there are recommendations to have multiple witnesses in such confrontations. Jesus mentioned it in regard to judging others (John 8:17). Paul reminded the Corinthians to have two or three witnesses in dealing with their troublemakers (2 Corinthians 13:1). Paul gave the same advice to Timothy when accusing an elder of wrongdoing (1 Timothy 5:19). These passages all have their roots in the Old Testament where in Deuteronomy 19:15 it says, "A single witness shall not rise up against a man on account of any iniquity or any sin which he has committed; on the evidence of two or three witnesses a matter shall be confirmed."

There is an important principal here. A truthful assessment needs to be confirmed by more than one person. As individuals, we can be inaccurate or unbalanced in our assessments of situations or others. As a matter of fact, there are studies showing how inaccurate eyewitness accounts can be in a court of law although such testimonies are provided by sincere people.

The inaccuracies of a single witness should give us reason for pause when we begin to question someone about their actions. Prayerful consideration should be made before initiating this process of confrontation. But by all means follow the process in the given order. Reversing the order—talking to others before talking to the individual involved—is essentially nothing more than verbal defecation. This can create a mess for the individual in question as well as for others in the church as they may needlessly take sides regarding an issue or an individual when there may not be a problem after all.

Confrontation is always difficult. Furthermore, in our postmodern era in which individuals tend to have a non-absolute view of truth, confrontation may be culturally inappropriate and therefore avoided. Confrontation is necessary, though, because we all go off track in some way or another. Many of the New Testament epistles were prompted by the need of the apostles to confront wayward or uninformed disciples. When the apostles saw a problem they took action to bring it to the attention of those involved for their own good.

Some might say this process involves passing judgment on someone and therefore should not be done. These folks are usually referring to Jesus' words in the Sermon on the Mount—"Do not judge so that you will not be judged." But this statement means we should not be harshly critical or condemning of others.[3] Furthermore, Jesus Himself said, "Do not judge according to appearance, but judge with righteous judgment" (John 7:24). When we do confront someone, Paul provided these words of caution: "Brethren, even if anyone is caught in any trespass, you who are spiritual, *restore such a one in a spirit of gentleness; each one looking to yourself, so that you too will not be tempted*" (Galatians 6:1).

During the winter when the bees leave the hive to go on a cleansing flight they risk dying from exposure to the cold. Just as bees are taking a risk when they tend to their personal business in a proper manner, so too must believers take risks when taking care of interpersonal business. Confrontation can be difficult. But it is a part of doing business that is necessary to maintain a healthy organization with growing individuals. Blessed is the man or woman who is loved enough by friends or family to be confronted for his or her own good.

Chapter 10

Guard Bees

One might be tempted to think that since all worker bees have stingers the specific function of guard duty is not necessary. But there are bees whose specific task it is to be on guard to protect the hive. They stand as a sentry or they will patrol near the entrance of the hive keeping an eye open for intruders. The intruders may be animals, such as mice, skunks or bears. Humans also are unwelcome guests in the hive. Other insects, such as ants, moths, hornets and even honeybees from other hives, may try to invade or attack.

Honeybees are not territorial in that they do not lay claim to certain areas containing blooming plants of interest. They do consider their hive to be theirs, however, and no one else's. These facts are substantiated by noting where honeybees will sting someone or something in relationship to their proximity to the hive. For example, they will rarely sting while away from the hive and foraging in the field. But when they are near to the hive, they will sting.[1] I have impressed friends by petting honeybees—

gently stroking them with my bare finger—as they were visiting flowers in our garden. (Warning: do not try this unless you are willing to risk being stung.) Needless to say, my friends initially thought I was nuts but later were amazed the bees either ignored me or simply flew away. I would never try that stunt anywhere near a hive.

When a bee stings, the barbs on the stinger secure it to the target or victim. The bee will then pull away from the location of the sting. In so doing, the stinger, along with a poison sac and the small intestines, are ripped from the bee's body. Even though detached from the bee, the stinger apparatus will continue to pump venom into the victim for several minutes.[2] The bee, because she lost her intestines, will die usually within an hour.

It was once thought that guard bees were generally the oldest worker bees. One can determine the relative age of a bee by appearances as younger bees typically have more fuzz on their bodies than do older bees and younger bees have fuller wings.[3] The reasoning behind older bees serving as guards was based upon the condition of their wings. As the bees went about their business of gathering supplies earlier in life, their wings became somewhat tattered and worn from countless foraging flights. As their wings deteriorated, they became less and less efficient to carry supplies back to the hive. Thus it made sense that they could spend their final days serving the colony by patrolling the hive entrance on foot. Recent studies, though, seem to indicate guard duty is performed about midway through their lives, and it is perhaps the last job they have as a "hive bee" before becoming a "field bee" and spending the rest of their lives foraging for supplies.[4]

On several occasions I have observed guard bees in action. From a few feet away I would watch the comings and goings of the bees. The entrance to a hive is very congested. Scout bees are busily launching or landing in fulfilling their reconnaissance role. Weary foragers are returning with their goods while those who just unloaded their cargo set out yet again. There are bees standing near the entrance fanning their wings to provide ventilation to aid in the important job of climate control. But despite all of the activity one sometimes is able to see the guard bees at work.

When a bee would land at the hive entrance a guard bee would race to meet it face-to-face. The two bees would stand still for a few seconds. The guard bee would perform what looked to be a pat-down much like what is done by a policeman to an apprehended suspect. The guard bee would pat the returning bee with its antennae and its front legs. The guard bee was not looking for a concealed weapon but was "sniffing" the other bee with the sensors on its antennae.[5] Each colony has a unique scent. The guard bee was verifying that the returning bee belonged to that hive by checking its scent. Once satisfied with the identification check, the guard bee would let the other bee pass. The guard bee would then busily chase another bee that had landed nearby and had tried to enter the hive while she was still checking the first bee. The guard bee caught up with the impatient bee and repeated the identification check.

This guard bee's job seemed hopelessly futile as dozens of bees were coming and going every minute. Nevertheless she faithfully went about her duty. She was not the only guard bee on duty but was the only one I happened to observe. The larger the colony, the larger the guard force available to patrol the entrance.

Guard bees protect the hive from intruders and the dangers they bring. When a threat is detected, guard bees release a scent, or pheromone, that alerts the whole colony to the potential threat. Once alerted, all of the bees go to battle stations. From personal experience it is quite intimidating when an entire colony is in an agitated state—the entire hive hums, and dozens of bees take flight to attack. The use of smoke by beekeepers interferes with this alarm scent, and therefore the hive usually remains calm (or at least goes into a state of confusion) while the beekeeper performs his inspections.

Once while inspecting my hive I noticed the bees seemed to be in a particularly bad mood. As I slowly took the hive apart to conduct an inspection, I observed that more bees than normal were buzzing around me. Even though I had smoked the beehive prior to starting my inspection, I picked up my smoker to give them another dose. But my smoker was being temperamental and was nearly extinguished. This failed attempt to re-smoke the bees seemed only to further agitate them as more bees took flight and the sound of their collective buzzing grew louder.

With the bees agitated and my smoker of little use I briefly entertained the idea of quickly closing up the hive and coming back another day. Instead I convinced myself to proceed and finish my inspection and, as the saying goes, "so much for common sense." The guard bees would make me pay for my poor decision.

The guard bees led the charge to attack. Evidently it mattered little to them that I was their owner, let alone several thousand times their size. Their attacks were relentless and grew in intensity. Bees were bouncing off of my veil as they tried to sting my face. They were also landing on all parts of my body. Even though I was suited up in my protective gear, I was still being stung. They would attempt to sting me but were actually thrusting their stingers into my pants, shirt and gloves. When I would move in certain ways, these articles of clothing would be pulled tight against my skin. When this occurred with a stinger lodged in those areas, the stinger would come through the fabric and prick my skin. Ouch!

Needless to say I was quite happy when I finally finished my inspection. When I was removing my protective gear and checked myself, I had received about a dozen stings on my hands, forearms and thighs. Fortunately, when a stinger pierces through fabric, not all of the venom reaches the skin, and therefore the wounds were not as painful as they could have been. When I then looked at my gear which I had just removed, I could not help but notice over fifty stingers still embedded in my two gloves! The bees were only doing what was natural for them to do to protect the hive. But it was the guard bees that sounded the alarm and led the charge.

Just as the guard bees are to protect the hive, so also are elders, or church leaders, to protect their congregations. When we look into the New Testament we note the early churches had elders. We also note there are multiple elders at the churches. The apostle Paul appointed elders at the churches he visited (Acts 14:23). Paul was evidently so convinced of the important function elders perform within the church that he directed Titus to also appoint elders "in every city" under his responsibility (Titus 1:5). The concept of elders originated in Old Testament times when cities were led by the most experienced (oldest) men. At the time of Christ synagogues (local houses of worship) were led by men call "elders." Paul utilized this existing leadership structure in the churches he started during his travels.[6]

Depending upon the version of the Bible one uses, the terms *bishop* (1 Timothy 3:1), *overseer* (Titus 1:7) and *elder* (Titus 1:5) may be observed. These words appear to be used interchangeably by Paul. Also, some churches use the term *pastor* when referring to elders. Regardless of the title, Paul established the qualifications for these leaders. They were reputable men who managed their families well. An elder was to be "above reproach as God's steward, not self-willed, not quick-tempered, not addicted to wine, not pugnacious, not fond of sordid gain, but hospitable, loving what is good, sensible, just, devout, self-controlled, holding fast the faithful word which is in accordance with the teaching, so that he will be able both to exhort in sound doctrine and to refute those who contradict" (Titus 1:7-9).

Notice the purpose for elders that Paul gives: "so that he will be able both to exhort in sound doctrine and to refute those who contradict." The elders were key individuals in promoting the truth of the faith and in refuting those who contradicted the truth. They are to protect Christ's followers from being influenced by harmful false teachings. This task given to church leaders, then and now, is not to be taken lightly. Hebrews 13:17 reinforces the gravity of this role by instructing believers to "obey your leaders and submit to them, *for they keep watch over your souls as those who will give an account.*"

Given the seriousness of this role within the church, elders need to be constantly on the alert and monitoring what is going on within their church. They need to be as diligent as the guard bee mentioned above that checked the identity of the bees coming into the hive. Elders can perform their roles in several ways. For example, they need to closely monitor the pastor's messages for accuracy and clarity. Sometimes even well-intending pastors or priests can misspeak or cause confusion on some points. The elders also need to be in touch with the church members to see if they are being negatively impacted or led astray by sources outside the church. This requires diligence to be personally involved in the lives of the congregants to be able to assess their condition.

To do this job well, these leaders first must meet the qualifications put forth in Scripture. In addition to what Paul told Titus, Paul provided Timothy with a few more qualifications: elders must be able to teach and cautions that they should not be new converts (1 Timothy 3:1-7). Peter weighed in on this subject also and emphasized the importance of having proper motives. "Therefore, I exhort the elders among you ... shepherd the flock of God among you, exercising oversight not under compulsion, but voluntarily, according to the will of God; and not for sordid gain, but with eagerness; nor yet as lording it over those allotted to your charge, but proving to be examples to the flock" (1 Peter 5:1-3).

Strongly implied in these passages is the notion that elders need to be well versed in the Scriptures so they can promote the truth as well as recognize error or counterfeits. Also implied is the willingness or ability to confront. Just as the guard bees were willing to confront me as I violated their home, so also should elders be willing to actively and, if necessary, aggressively confront individuals for the sake of protecting those under their care and supervision.

When a guard bee attacks an animal or person who is threatening their hive, it is no small act for the bee. When it stings an intruder, the bee's stinger and small intestine are ripped from its body. By inflicting a sting, the guard bee is sacrificing its life to protect others. Elders of a church may not be called upon to lay down their lives for their church. But the ability of an elder to fulfill his scriptural duties has spiritual life or death consequences.

Obviously, not everyone in a church is an elder. What about those of us who are not elders? What is our response to these leaders? First Timothy 5:17 says elders who rule well are worthy of honor. Evidently

Paul thought elders should be honored based upon how well they performed their roles and not based solely upon their title or their position. Therefore, while elders watch over the flock's well-being, the flock is to assess the elders' performance. No one should be afforded any special treatment or respect based solely upon their title or position. Those in positions of authority bear a heavy burden of responsibility to fulfill the tasks to which they are called.

Another response of church members to their elders is obedience. As was cited above, Hebrews 13:17 directs believers to "obey your leaders and submit to them." The words *obey* and *submit* are not popular in our culture today. But this is how the whole verse reads: "Obey your leaders and submit to them, for they keep watch over your souls as those who will give an account. *Let them do this with joy and not with grief, for this would be unprofitable for you.*" The second sentence clearly indicates there is an interactive relationship occurring between the leaders and laity that can be beneficial or detrimental to both parties. When there is cooperation within the church, the leaders will have a sense of joy or fulfillment in performing their role on behalf of the laity, and the laity in turn will profit in the sense that they are being protected from harm and experiencing growth in their spiritual lives. If there is no cooperation, then a problem exists that grieves the leaders and thwarts the progress of the laity. It is in everyone's best long-term interest that there is willing cooperation among all members of a church.

If the church leaders are faithfully fulfilling their roles and it is clear they are acting in a loving manner with the church's best interest at heart, then obedience and submission should not be a burdensome task. Perhaps we can learn from the honeybees. When the guard bees signal the presence of danger and lead the charge to repel an intruder, then it is in the best interest of every member of the colony to mobilize and join the charge. The guard bee's role as protector of the hive is paramount for the colony's survival. Leaders within the church are responsible for those under their care. Those persons being cared for need to share in the responsibility of their own well being as well as that of their fellow-believers. Coordination and cooperation are essential for the common good, both with bees and with believers.

Chapter 11

Thieves

Honeybees usually have a good reputation because they are known as being hard working and industrious. We have all heard of the expression "busy as a bee" applied to someone who is diligent and busily goes about his or her activities. Some like to associate themselves with these traits. In fact, my town's logo includes an image of a honeybee and a skep. Despite their generally good reputation, though, honeybees do have a dark side.

When a hive is weak, it is often subject to attack from, among other things, honeybees from a neighboring hive. These attacking honeybees are called robbers. A weak hive will try to defend itself. Eventually, however, the numerous and persistent robbers will win and have their way with the weakened hive. The robbers have only one goal—honey. Free food in nature is a rare occurrence for bees. When it does occur, the bees go wild. Just as blood in the water starts a feeding frenzy among sharks, so will unguarded honey stimulate robbing. In a matter of hours an ill-protected hive can be completely emptied of its honey supply. It may seem strange that social insects like honeybees, which work together for the greater good of their own colony, would take advantage of another colony. Evidently for bees, when it comes to survival, it is every colony for itself.

In addition to the frenzied buzz of activity surrounding a hive that is being robbed, there is another sign that things are amiss. Being overloaded with honey, robber bees will crawl up the outside of the hive to have sufficient altitude from which to launch so they will be able to take flight to return to their hive.[1]

If beekeepers are aware that robbing is taking place within their apiary, they will try to stop the plundering. The beekeepers will try to close any openings or cracks between the supers of a weak hive and will reduce the size of the entrance to give the guard bees a better chance to defend their hive. Guard bees know which bees belong to their hive and which ones do not. With a smaller entrance the guard bees can better control access and restrict intruders from entering. The beekeeper is not necessarily trying to help the weakened hive as much as he is simply trying to prevent an ongoing riot within the apiary.[2] Robbers could be coming from multiple hives. The more robbing that takes place, the more excited the robbers will become, and thus there could be an upward spiral of robbing that could victimize more than just the originally targeted weak hive.

Robbing can be inadvertently initiated by beekeepers. All that is needed to spark robbing is the presence of honey. When beekeepers inspect their hives, combs containing honey can be damaged in the process. The damaged comb can leak honey onto the ground or on the exterior of the inspected hive. If the beekeeper does not quickly reassemble the hive and do his best to clean up the spilt honey, bees from neighboring hives will catch the scent of the honey. These bees will attack and rob the hive while it is disassembled during the beekeeper's inspection. Once they whet their appetite with the taste of free food, the robber bees may continue to attack the inspected hive even after it is reassembled, or they may attack some other hive in the apiary that is weak.

There is another way beekeepers can initiate robbing. This can occur when beekeepers are in the process of removing honey from a hive. When a beekeeper determines the supers are full of honey, there are two ways to remove the supers. The usual method is when the bees are brushed, blown or smoked out of or off the desired frames and supers. This causes a lot of bees to become agitated when they are dislodged from the supers, and as a result a lot of bees are flying around. Another disadvantage of this method is that it is nearly impossible to get all of the bees out of the honey-filled frames and supers.

To avoid disturbing the bees while removing nearly all of them from the supers, beekeepers can use a second method. This method involves installing a board with a trap door beneath the supers containing the honey which will be removed. The bees in the desired supers will exit the supers by going down through the trap door. This door allows the bees to move in only one direction. Thus, the bees can exit the supers but cannot re-enter. Therefore, over the course of about two days, the desired supers are almost completely free of bees. The beekeeper needs only to take off the top cover from the hive and remove the desired supers. Once the supers are out of the hive, the board with the trap door is removed, and the top cover is then placed atop the hive.

There are two drawbacks to this method. One, the beekeeper has to enter the hive twice—once to install the board with the trap door beneath the supers and the second time to remove the supers and the board. The other drawback is that the beekeeper must be absolutely sure of one thing regarding the supers which will be removed—these supers must not have any openings large enough for a bee to enter from the outside. If there is an opening, robber bees will find it. While the native bees are exiting the supers through the trap door, the robbers will remove the honey through the unguarded opening. When the beekeeper returns to retrieve the supers, he will be disappointed to find the supers completely empty.

The bottom line of this chapter is that good bees can become bandits. They will not hesitate to become intruders and enter another hive and deplete it of its life-sustaining food. Churches, like beehives, can also be victimized by intruders. These intruders can come in different forms. They can be individuals who are looking out only for themselves. Also, they can be people who are spreading errant teachings or philosophies.

Unfortunately there are those who find their way into our churches with their own twisted agenda.

There are pedophiles who try to volunteer to "help" in the children's ministries. Churches now need to take various precautions in screening those volunteering in these ministries. Also, churches have had to implement precautions or rules for their volunteers. For example, there must be at least two adults present at all times such that at no time will an adult be one-on-one with a child.

In large churches there are potential kidnappers who would like to take advantage of the confusion surrounding the dropping off and picking up of kids from the church's child care. Churches circumvent this problem by the dehumanizing (but necessary) method of assigning matching numbers to parents and kids to ensure the right kid leaves with the right adults.

Then there are the free loaders. These people are parasites that take advantage of the kindness and generosity of the church and its members. There is always a fine line between helping those in need and enabling people to remain irresponsible. Perhaps one of the toughest jobs in any church is the head of the compassion ministry. Trying to determine if a true need exists or if something else is at play is never easy. Generally speaking, people want to help others in need. It is both humane and Christian to do so. But no one wants to be taken advantage of, especially when other legitimate needs are readily apparent and the needs will always outstrip the available resources.

In the cases just mentioned, the harm is emotional, physical and financial. Such ill-purposed people cause harm to the innocent and unsuspecting. The reputation of the victimized church and the integrity of Christianity can also be tarnished. But a greater threat is posed by individuals or philosophies that undermine the core teachings of the faith.

Paul reminded the Galatians about some bad characters that had entered their midst. "But it was because of the false brethren secretly brought in, who had sneaked in to spy out our liberty which we have in Christ Jesus, in order to bring us into bondage" (Galatians 2:4). Paul's letter to the Galatians reminded them about the sole sufficiency of faith in Christ's work on the cross for their salvation. The Judaizers had evidently infiltrated their ranks in order to add the keeping of the Mosaic Law as an essential part to their salvation. One thing in particular they were trying to get the Galatian Christians to do was become circumcised (Galatians 5:1-15). There may also have been pressure regarding dietary restraints (Galatians 2:12) and observing special days (Galatians 4:10). But the book of Galatians clearly puts forth that one's right standing before God comes through faith alone in Christ and is completely separate from the law.

Jude, in his small and almost completely neglected epistle, gave warning about intruders. When Jude set out to write his epistle, he wanted to write about good things; but he had to deal with a problem. "Beloved, while I was making every effort to write you about our common salvation, I felt the necessity to write to you appealing that you contend earnestly for the faith which was once for all handed down to the saints. For certain persons have crept in unnoticed, those who were long beforehand marked out for this condemnation, ungodly persons who turn the grace of our God into licentiousness and deny our only Master and Lord, Jesus Christ" (Jude 3-4). Later Jude writes that those who had crept in even participated in the church's love feasts (the celebration of the Lord's Supper). Jude goes on to further describe these people and their actions, thus warning his audience of the dangers these people posed. Encouraging people to live immoral lives, as well as denying the deity of Christ, would have been devastating to the faith of Jude's audience.

John also wrote of nonbelievers who had been a part of the churches under his care. "Children, it is the last hour; and just as you heard that antichrist is coming, even now many antichrists have appeared; from this we know that it is the last hour. They went out from us, but they were not really of us; for if they had been of us, they would have remained with us; but they went out, so that it would be shown that they all are not of us" (1 John 2:18-19). Evidently those that had left gave the false appearance of being genuine believers. In reality they were agents of Satan that had been fellowshipping among the flock. We can only imagine the extent of their evil influence.

Of course, the first saboteur within Christianity was Judas. He may have been more astute than the other apostles in terms of his understanding Jesus was not going to establish a political kingdom at that time. Although we do not know exactly what Judas understood about Jesus' earthly mission, it is apparent he no longer wanted to follow Him. That being the case, Judas decided to cash in on his disappointment by betraying Jesus.

But as can be seen through these New Testament examples, the early church had its hands full dealing with threats from individuals or groups who had entered their midst. These people threatened to undermine or corrupt the life-giving truth of the gospel. Christians in the early church, as well as Christians today, need to be aware of these threats and respond accordingly.

Often times a lot of the problems today stem from well-intended Christians who overemphasize one tenet of Scripture and thus create imbalance. There are those who expound upon the demonstrative spiritual gifts such as speaking in tongues. There are those who, in an effort to emphasize the importance of faith, become presumptuous of God's will by touting a "name it and claim it" message. Then there are those who promote a "health, wealth and prosperity" gospel. All of these ideas have at least a thread of scriptural truth. But they need to be carefully investigated, explained, nuanced and applied. It detracts from the overall effectiveness of any ministry when the pastor or other church leaders have to take time to address these tangents at the expense of the tending to the church's core business of building God's kingdom.

Problems also enter through the front door of a church in the form of the very people the church is trying to reach. Many non-Christians who visit a church today will bring with them their own brand of spirituality. With today's cultural emphasis on diversity and inclusion, however, much of what is brought into the church by these individuals is clearly contrary to orthodox Christianity. The threats to the core values of Christianity are many. A common one is the claim that there are many ways to God, of which Jesus is but one. Another is that Jesus was only a man who happened to have special insights regarding God. Another is that mankind in general is not so bad and thus does not need a Savior because we will all end up in heaven anyway. Related to this one is the notion that the answer to our individual and global problems lies within each one of us and we can save ourselves. Of course, the underlying premise of these views is that the Scriptures are not authoritative or, at the very least, are too subjective to convey any meaningful truth in today's world.

The church that attracts nonbelievers is in a dilemma. Larger churches tend to attract more visitors because they have more programs and activities to offer than smaller churches. Therefore, the larger churches probably face this issue more often than smaller churches, but any church is susceptible and must therefore be on guard. How does the church go about communicating with those who have these views without being too heavy handed and thus driving them away?

In addition to the smorgasbord approach to spirituality that nonbelievers bring with them, these people tend to be very community oriented. They want to belong to a group. Therefore, interpersonal relationships are very important to them in order to feel a sense of belonging. What does this mean for the church? It means two things. First, the days of believing first and then belonging are past. The reverse is now true. Non-Christians want to belong first before they consider believing. The church needs to be aware of this change. The second thing for the church to realize is that the days of sharing the "Four Spiritual Laws" and tent revivals or crusades is of very limited value when it comes to introducing someone to Christ. The *message* of the "Four Spiritual Laws" will always remain foundational. The *method* of using the "Four Spiritual Laws" is fading. In order to lead non-Christians to Christ in today's culture, churches and believers must be willing to invest in the long term. It will take many hours of building bridges of friendship. It will take place at school, over dinners, before and after movies, or during the commute to and from the office. Believers will need to be open and genuine as they share their lives. It may take a lot of work before any progress is made. But apart from the mysterious work of the Holy Spirit nothing will happen. Therefore, much laboring in prayer will also be necessary.

Just as a hive must be strong to protect itself from robber bees, so too the church must be strong to deal with the variety of threats it will face. If a hive does not have a sufficient guard force, it will be vulnerable to thieves and lose its precious reserves of honey. Without a supply of honey the hive will be doomed to starvation when winter comes. If a church does not have enough mature well-grounded believers in its midst, that church will be ill-prepared to identify or respond to unbiblical or heretical views that find their way into the congregation. The message of the gospel is at stake. Since a pastor cannot be everywhere monitoring what goes on in Sunday school classes or small groups, it is imperative that he is continually discipling those who can also protect the flock from the evil one.

Jesus warned His disciples saying, "The thief comes only to steal and kill and destroy" (John 10:10).

Chapter 12

Belonging

One day while channel surfing, I came across an educational show that exposed children to various features of nature. This particular episode happened to be about honeybees. Being a big fan of bees, I had to put down the remote, sit back and watch. Usually, when I watch something on TV about bees it ends up being a refresher of what I already know. Much of this episode was no exception. One segment of this show, however, covered an aspect I had not seen explained before on TV.

This one segment of the show was explaining how bees belong to specific hives. If they try to enter another hive, they will be prohibited from doing so by the guard bees of that hive. This episode showed an apiary of several hives that were located only a few feet from each other. Despite being excellent navigators, honeybees can go slightly off course when returning to their hive. If there are several hives in close proximity, a small navigational error will result in a bee trying to enter a hive other than its own. To minimize this problem, beekeepers will sometimes paint their hives different colors to aid the bees in recognizing their home.

During this portion of the show the camera focused on a struggle that was occurring at the entrance to one of the hives. There was a wrestling match taking place between two bees. One was a guard bee, and the other was a bee from another hive. The guard bee would try to push the visitor away from the entrance. But the visitor was stubborn and would push back against the guard as she tried to head toward the entrance of the hive she thought was hers.

The struggle continued for a few seconds until another guard bee arrived to help repel the persistent visitor. The two guard bees together were successful in pushing the visitor away from the entrance and off the edge of the landing board. Once thrown off the edge, though, the visitor revved up her wings to stop her fall. She then hovered around the landing board for a few seconds. Not taking "No" for an answer, she landed and again attempted to enter the hive.

Upon landing, she was greeted by more guard bees which were more than happy to push her back to the edge and throw her overboard again. The expelled visitor again broke her fall and continued to hover around the landing board once more. When she landed, the welcome committee unceremoniously greeted her yet again by booting her off the edge. This cycle of landing, wrestling, ejecting and hovering continued several more times. One would think the visitor would get the message and begin to look for her own hive.

Bee Parables

Evidently the guard bees were becoming increasingly annoyed by this persistent visitor. Patience was wearing thin toward this outsider. When the visitor landed again, one of the guard bees jumped on top of her and grabbed hold. The guard bee then unsheathed her stinger and impaled the visitor with her lethal venom. Both the visitor and the guard bee rolled together and plunged off the landing board to the ground below where both died—the visitor from the sting's venom and the guard from losing her intestines when she impaled her stinger into the visitor.

It seems odd that this type of behavior would exist among bees. One would naturally expect guard bees to protect the hive from other insect species such as moths, ants or hornets. But to take such drastic action against a member of one's own species seems to be somewhat extreme especially in light of the fact that honeybees are social insects. From the guard bee's perspective, however, a foreign bee could be a spy or a robber from another hive that is attempting to steal their precious honey. Regardless of the visitor's intentions, the guards usually will not take any chances and will stop all foreigners from entering. As seen above, no matter how persistently the visiting bee was when she attempted to enter another hive, she was stopped and ultimately lost her life. Nothing she could do on her own would allow her to become a member of another hive.

Each colony of bees has its own unique scent. This scent provides a means of identification for each of the members of that particular colony. The guard bees recognized the visiting bee as a foreigner based upon her unique scent. The visiting bee could probably detect that the scent of the guard bees' hive was different from her own. Evidently, however, she was depending upon her own navigational skills to guide her back to her home. Her error in navigation and her refusal to recognize she was at the wrong hive were fatal mistakes.

Despite bees' natural reluctance to accept foreigners as cited above, beekeepers are able to merge bees from two different colonies. Beekeepers usually do this to combine two weak colonies which are struggling in order to form one strong colony. Also, beekeepers simply add the bees of an otherwise doomed weaker colony with a stronger colony which can always use more workers. The combining of colonies is usually done during two times of the year. The first occurs in the early spring when beekeepers are trying to manage the population of their hives so that they will peak at the proper time to take advantage of the seasonal nectar flow. The other occurrence is in the fall in an effort to ensure the colonies have enough bees to maintain an adequate population to generate sufficient warmth during the cold winter months.

Combining colonies is not very difficult to do. A beekeeper will remove the roof and inner cover from one hive. He then will place a sheet of ordinary newspaper over the exposed top super. Next he will stack the super(s) of another hive onto the top super of the first hive with only the sheet of newspaper separating the supers of these two colonies of bees. The beekeeper will close the combined hive by placing the inner cover and roof on the topmost super. The beekeeper's work is done. He will walk away and let nature take its course.

Both colonies of bees, the one above the newspaper and the one below, will begin to chew through the newspaper. Without the separation created by the newspaper the two colonies would recognize the presence of a foreign scent, and both groups would go to battle stations. There would be all-out war between the two colonies if it were not for the newspaper. As the two colonies begin to chew through the newspaper, however, their scents will begin to mix. As the scents mix, the two groups become less and less hostile toward each other. By the time the newspaper has been shredded to the point where members of the two colonies can physically interact, all hostility is gone. The once separate colonies are now one. The only thing left to be decided is which queen will reign. Either the bees somehow decide which queen stays or goes (dies), or the queens will have a fight to the death. Usually the stronger healthier queen wins the fight. This is the optimum outcome for the colony and for the beekeeper to have the best possible queen.

One time I used this method to combine two groups of bees. Actually I had captured a swarm of bees that had left my hive. I did not want to lose a large portion of my bees as the peak of the honey-making season was fast approaching. I removed the roof and inner cover from my hive. I placed a sheet of newspaper on the exposed top super. I then stacked an empty super on top of the newspaper.

When the swarm left the hive, they had gathered in a cluster about the size of a volleyball and were hanging from a nearby low branch. My wife helped me collect the swarm. One of us placed a bucket under the cluster, and the other gave the branch a sudden forceful shake. The bees fell from the branch into the bucket. (I remember being surprised at the weight of the cluster of bees in the bucket.) We took the bucket of bees back to the hive and literally poured them into the empty super I had just placed on top of the hive. The inner cover and roof were installed. We then waited and hoped to see if the swarm would stay or if the bees would try to swarm again.

The next day I returned to the hive to see if the bees had chewed through the newspaper so the swarm would be reunited with their former hive-mates. Because an unfolded sheet of newspaper has a larger area than the footprint of a super, there were a few inches of newspaper sticking out on all sides from between the top super and the empty super I had added. When I removed the roof and inner cover, I was expecting to see several small holes in the newspaper where the bees had tunneled through to escape the top super and be joined with the rest of the hive. To my surprise, there was not one shred of evidence that a sheet of newspaper had ever existed between these two supers! When I removed the empty super, there was the sheet of newspaper with a perfectly rectangular cut-out in the middle exactly matching the dimensions of the super. Since the colors of bees are black and gold, I should have known their favorite team was the Pittsburgh Steelers. Therefore, using a sheet of newspaper from the *Philadelphia Enquirer* sports section covering the Eagles probably agitated the bees into a wild frenzy that prompted them to totally destroy the newspaper.

The point in this chapter is to realize that bees typically cannot join another colony based upon their own efforts. The beekeeper must take the necessary steps in order to combine bees of different colonies into one unified colony. Just as the bees must depend upon the beekeeper to join them with another colony, so also individuals must solely rely upon Jesus to be accepted into God's forever family. Individuals can do nothing on their own to merit eternal life. There is no other way to heaven. We must trust completely in what Jesus has done for us.

Jesus made this point in John 3:16. "For God so loved the world, that He gave His only begotten Son, that whoever *believes* in Him shall not perish, but have eternal life." Note that believing is the only requirement Jesus mentions. Believing is more than an intellectual assent. Belief, or faith, within the biblical context can better be understood as active trust or reliance. In other words, I can *believe* a chair will support me, but it does me no good until I demonstrate *faith* by actually sitting (trusting) in the chair. Likewise, believing in the existence of God is much different from trusting God.[1]

The apostle Paul is also clear regarding the necessity of faith for salvation. "For by *grace* you have been saved through *faith*; and *that not of yourselves*, it is the *gift* of God; *not as a result of works*, so that no one may boast" (Ephesians 2:8-9).

Several words are important in these verses. *Grace*, the New Testament equivalent of *loving kindness*, refers to God's initiative of demonstrating kindness and compassion to fallen mankind. God's grace is unmerited, but it prompts a response that leads to restoration of humanity with Himself.[2] Thus, in the context of Ephesians 2:8-9, *grace* is simply God's undeserved favor that is freely offered to all and can be received only through *faith*.

Faith, as was stated above, involves action. *Faith* is more than mere intellectual assent to the truth of the gospel message. It also involves a conscious act of the will to rely completely upon the Savior. *Faith* that leads to salvation is a trust that is placed in Jesus Christ and Him alone. There is no other way. Jesus Himself said He is the only way (John 14:6). No doubt there will be those who dislike the exclusiveness of this position. But let's apply some simple logic. One of Jesus' claims was that He is God (for example, John 10:30, 14:23, and 17:21). Either this is true, or it is not. If it is true, then everything Jesus said has absolute authority including the statement that He is the only way. If Jesus is not God, then He was either a convincing fraud or He was insane.[3] If you have concluded Jesus is not who He claimed to be, then I respect your decision. But if that is your conclusion, then I must challenge you to discard Christianity from the smorgasbord of contending world religions because it is based upon a leader who was either a liar or a lunatic. Do not fool yourself into thinking God will accept *your faith* because you are open-minded and hedging your bet by embracing all religions. That is not saving faith. If you have concluded Jesus is not God, then logically you must throw Christianity upon the scrap heap of other failed or fraudulent ideas that have originated in the human mind. If you conclude He is God, then you are logically obliged to discard all other religions because Jesus is the only way.

And that not of yourselves and *not as a result of works* are phrases that indicate salvation cannot be acquired by merit nor can it be earned. There is probably a temptation by some to discount this. After all, some may think they are not that bad of a person, and it would seem quite plausible to be able to compensate for their shortcomings and sins they have committed. When it comes to personal self-assessment, however, there is a tendency for people to think more highly of themselves than they should.[4] Another thing to bear in mind is that in understanding sin it is not the *quantity* that matters but the *quality*. For example, one single spore of the bacteria that causes American foul brood disease can germinate and spread to destroy an entire colony of bees. Also, one single trace of the AIDS virus can likewise spread throughout an otherwise healthy individual and overcome the immune system and result in death. One is either contaminated by sin or not. Unfortunately, all of us are contaminated (Romans 3:23), and we all are in need of a cure that is well beyond our own capabilities. The penalty of sin is death—separation from God (Romans 6:23). Either we can pay the penalty ourselves, or we can trust in Jesus' death as payment for the penalty.

There also may be those who think eternal life is the result of believing in Jesus and doing good works.

These individuals may point to James 2:20-21 as evidence to support their view: "But are you willing to recognize, you foolish fellow, that faith without works is useless? Was not Abraham our father justified by works when he offered up Isaac his son on the altar?"

A quick review of history can clarify this point. When one looks back at the life of Abraham, ask yourself, "When did God declare him to be righteous?" It was when God made a covenant with Abraham and his descendants in Genesis 15. The offering up of Isaac occurred later in Genesis (chapter 22). Abraham was already righteous in God's eyes when he went to sacrifice Isaac.

James and Paul both used the word *justified* in their writings. James used it to mean *to show to be righteous* whereas Paul's meaning is *to declare a sinner righteous before God*.[5] Furthermore, James and Paul are using the word *faith* differently. James is using the concept of faith in a generic sense to refer to a particular belief system such as monotheism whereas Paul uses faith to mean a personal trust in Christ.[6] These explanations are obvious when one realizes the book of James is very practically oriented in its emphasis and is primarily concerned that Christians practice proper living. Paul, in his writings, is primarily emphasizing correct teaching.[7]

Eternal life is a *gift* from God. A gift is something someone *gives* to you. You do not earn a gift. A gift comes forth from the generosity of a giver. But a gift is not yours until you receive it. An offered gift is an unclaimed gift until it is received. If someone is handing you a gift, it does not come into your possession until you reach out and take it. In this case, God is the giver. God is offering an unearned, unmerited gift of eternal life to everyone. This wonderful gift is of no use unless it is received.

Titus 3:3-7 explains and sums up this discussion well. "It wasn't so long ago that we ourselves were stupid and stubborn, dupes of sin, ordered every which way by our glands, going around with a chip on our shoulder, hated and hating back. But when God, our kind and loving Savior God, stepped in, he saved us from all that. It was all his doing; we had nothing to do with it. He gave us a good bath, and we came out of it new people, washed inside and out by the Holy Spirit. Our Savior Jesus poured out new life so generously. God's gift has restored our relationship with him and given us back our lives. And there's more life to come—an eternity of life! You can count on this." (*The Message*)

If you receive God's gift of eternal life, this does not mean you will be perfect or free from sin and its effects. As long as you are alive on this earth, you will be struggling with sin—yours and others. If believers sin, it does not change their standing in God's eyes. Romans 3:24 says believers are in a state of "being justified as a gift by His grace." Those who have trusted completely in Christ are guiltless in God's eyes. All sin in a believer's life—past, present and future—has been dealt with.[8] The debt of sin has been paid in full. This is truly good news!

This does not mean, however, that believers have a license to behave anyway they please and are free to live an immoral or self-centered life. A life genuinely touched by God's grace will be a transformed life. The transformation may be immediate in some instances, or it may be gradual; but nevertheless a transformation of attitudes and actions should occur as God's Spirit works within and through the believer. Believers have the responsibility to live pure lives. When believers stumble and sin, however, fellowship with God is broken, but their righteous standing before God does not change. We are still His precious children. Believers need only to confess their sin (1 John 1:9) to restore fellowship. Therefore, do not wallow in the guilt of your sins. Assess what's going on in your heart, repent and move on. God is gracious and will forgive.

Salvation is a gift that cannot be earned. Just as a bee cannot become a member of another hive by its own efforts and has to rely upon the beekeeper, neither can any of us enter God's family by our efforts. We must trust only in the Person and work of Jesus.

If you have never reached out and accepted God's gift, why not do so now?

Chapter 13

Honey

When one thinks of honeybees, one's next thought is about honey!

Honey is the bees' most familiar product for mankind. It is also the major food source for bees. Honey is their source of carbohydrates whereas pollen provides their protein. Honey is the product of nectar, which is gathered from flowers, and enzymes that are added by the bees. Nectar is basically diluted sugar water that is secreted by flowers. When bees are gathering honey, they tend to prioritize the flowers they visit starting with those containing the most nectar then visiting others with less. Depending upon the time of year and location, bees sometimes do not have much choice regarding their food supply. Once they have located a source of food, bees will crawl into a flower and, with their long extendible tongues, siphon the nectar into their stomachs. Bees may visit up to a few hundred flowers to fill their "tanks" before returning to the hive.

While in the foraging bee's stomach, enzymes are added to the nectar, and some of the water is absorbed into the bee's body. Once back at the hive, this bee will give its stomach's contents to a house bee that will ingest the regurgitated mixture. While in this bee's stomach, more enzymes are added, and more water is removed. The house bee will then deposit the contents of its stomach into a cell for further moisture reduction.

The bees involved in this transfer process are obtaining some benefits. Many of the bees in a colony do not leave the hive on any given day because they are performing tasks within the hive. Like any creature, bees need water. These work-at-home bees, which are involved in this transfer process, are absorbing a small amount of water for hydration. Thus, this transfer process, which ultimately produces honey, benefits many colony members who are performing other vital tasks in the hive.

When this regurgitated substance is deposited into a cell it is called unripened honey. The bees must reduce the moisture content to about seventeen percent. The moisture content is lowered to the appropriate level by evaporation. Evaporation occurs as the bees will fan their wings to create air movement within the hive. When honey contains too much moisture, such as when it is in its unripened state, it can ferment and then be of no use to the bees. (No one needs bees that are flying under the influence. Speaking of fermentation, beer brewers use honey in the production of a beverage called *mead*.) Depending upon the available space, bees will spread the unripened honey over as much surface area of the cells as possible to expedite the evaporation process.[1] When the honey is at the proper moisture content, the bees will gather the ripened honey and store it for later use by placing a thin wax cap over the cell.

What exactly is honey? One source indicated that honey contains ash, calcium, chlorine, copper, iron, magnesium, manganese, phosphorus, potassium, silica, sodium, sulfur and trace elements.[2] Another source listed trace amounts of albumins, digestive enzymes, fats, formic and mallic acids, iron, lime, manganese, nitrogenous pollen, phosphorus, salts, sulfur and waxes.[3] (I assume that chemists and nutritionists may find the contents of honey to be interesting or important, but the bottom line is that it tastes good.) Regardless of its mineral content, honey is comprised of sugars (glucose and fructose) that require no digestion and can pass directly into the bloodstream from the digestive tract.[4]

Depending upon the source of the nectar, it has been estimated that bees may visit as many as one million flowers to make an ounce of honey. Also, it is estimated that a single bee will produce about one twelfth of an ounce of honey in its short lifetime. That amount of honey hardly seems worth the effort until it is multiplied by upwards of sixty thousand. Some beekeepers, who have their hives on a scale, have recorded weight gains of ten to twenty pounds per day during the peak nectar seasons! A strong colony of bees over the course of a year can produce a total of about three hundred pounds of honey. It is estimated that the distance flown by the bees to collect this amount of honey is equivalent to about two dozen round trips to the moon (about twelve million miles). The bees consume about one half of that amount during the honey-producing season (approximately from April to October) to feed themselves and the developing brood. The beekeeper will harvest about seventy-five pounds and the remaining seventy-five pounds will be stored in the hive to feed the bees from late fall to early spring.

Honey has some unique qualities in addition to being a sweetener. Honey has medicinal properties and was applied to wounds to fight infection. Honey is harmful to bacteria because of its acidity and a characteristic called high osmotic pressure. When honey contacts bacteria, the bacteria die as moisture is drawn out of the cells into the honey.[5] Because of its effect on bacteria, honey can be used as a preservative of sorts. Honey that is made and stored properly can last indefinitely. Honey has been found in jars that have been unearthed in archeological digs that remained good after twenty-six hundred years.[6] You may have thrown out a jar of old honey thinking it was no longer useable because it had crystallized. If slowly and carefully warmed, crystallized honey will return to its liquid form ready for use. But excessively overheating honey may cause it to lose its flavor.

Mankind and honey have had some interesting times together down through history. There is indication that people gathered honey at least nine thousand years ago as recorded on rock paintings that depict people with rope ladders and baskets taking honey from colonies located on a cliff.[7] When Alexander the Great died in about 323 B.C., his body was placed in a casket filled with honey to preserve it for the long trip back to Alexandria.[8] Prior to Alexander the Great, in 401 B.C., a Greek army of mercenaries was passing through the Black Sea area. While there, they ate naturally toxic honey that bees had made from rhododendron nectar. Thousands of soldiers acted insane before becoming ill. In a few days they recovered and continued their journey. About four centuries later three Roman squadrons were offered this type of honey by the locals. The soldiers were then killed the following morning since they were too sick to defend themselves. This region where the Greeks and Romans had been affected by this honey was believed to be the home of Dionysis, the god of madness. Pliny, the Roman naturalist, noted that mead (beer) made with this type of honey was drunk because of its enhanced effect.[9]

Fortunately, only a few plants can produce the type of nectar mentioned above. But honey has been used by mankind for centuries. The demand for honey increased in the United States due to shipping effects caused by World War I, the hardships of the Great Depression and rationing that occurred during World War II. In recent years in the United States the annual honey crop has varied between about 160 and 250 million pounds.[10] Lower grades of honey are used in the baking industry because honey keeps baked goods fresher longer[11] while most of the rest is sold for consumer use.

The word *honey* is mentioned sixty-one times throughout the Bible. Probably the most well-known use of the word occurs in the Old Testament when referring to the Promised Land as "a land flowing with milk and honey." It is used several times in the Song of Solomon. Interestingly enough, it is used only four times in the New Testament—twice referring to John the Baptist's diet and twice in Revelation.

There is a reference to honey in Psalm 19:7-11 that is of interest.

> The law of the Lord is perfect, restoring the soul;
> The testimony of the Lord is sure, making wise the simple.
> The precepts of the Lord are right, rejoicing the heart;
> The commandment of the Lord is pure, enlightening the eyes.
> The fear of the Lord is clean, enduring forever;
> The judgments of the Lord are true; they are righteous altogether.
> They are more desirable than gold, yes, than much fine gold;
> *Sweeter also than honey and the drippings of the honeycomb.*
> Moreover, by them Your servant is warned;
> In keeping them there is great reward.

In this psalm David extols the Word of God by describing it with many complimentary adjectives and stating the benefits it brings. It is the reference to honey that is germane to this book. Just as honey is the essential food for bees, so God's Word is an important source of spiritual food for the followers of Christ.

Prayerfully consider the following Scriptures. Note how God's Word is described, the work it accomplishes and our recommended response to it.

> When Moses had finished speaking all these words to all Israel, he said to them, "Take to your heart all the words with which I am warning you today, which you shall command your sons to observe carefully, even *all the words of this law*. For it is not an idle word for you; *indeed it is your life*" (Deuteronomy 32:45-47).

> *This book of the law* shall not depart from your mouth, but you shall meditate on it day and night, so that you may be careful to do according to all that is written in it; for then you will make your way prosperous, and then you will have success (Joshua 1:8).

> *Your word* is a lamp to my feet and a light to my path (Psalm 119:105).

> "For My thoughts are not your thoughts, nor are your ways My ways," declares the Lord. "For as the heavens are higher than the earth, so are My ways higher than your ways and My thoughts than your thoughts. For as the rain and the snow come down from heaven, and do not return there without watering the earth

and making it bear and sprout, and furnishing seed to the sower and bread to the eater; so will *My word* be which goes forth from My mouth; it will not return to Me empty, without accomplishing what I desire, and without succeeding in the matter for which I sent it" (Isaiah 55:8-11).

But He answered and said, "It is written, 'Man shall not live on bread alone, but on every *word* that proceeds out of the mouth of God'" (Matthew 4:4).

Therefore everyone who hears *these words of Mine* and acts on them, may be compared to a wise man who built his house on the rock. And the rain fell, and the floods came, and the winds blew and slammed against that house; and yet it did not fall, for it had been founded on the rock. Everyone who hears *these words of Mine* and does not act on them, will be like a foolish man who built his house on the sand. The rain fell, and the floods came, and the winds blew and slammed against that house; and it fell—and great was its fall (Matthew 7:24-27).

But He said, "Blessed are those who hear the *word of God* and observe it" (Luke 11:28).

Let the *word of Christ* richly dwell within you (Colossians 3:16).

All *Scripture* is inspired by God and profitable for teaching, for reproof, for correction, for training in righteousness; so that the man of God may be adequate, equipped for every good work (2 Timothy 3:16-17).

But prove yourselves doers of the *word*, and not merely hearers who delude themselves (James 1:22).

Like newborn babies, long for the pure milk of the *word*, so that by it you may grow in respect to salvation (1 Peter 2:2).

I testify to everyone who hears the *words of the prophecy of this book*: if anyone adds to them, God will add to him the plagues which are written in this book; and if anyone takes away from the *words of the book of this prophecy*, God will take away his part from the tree of life and from the holy city, which are written in this book (Revelation 22:18-19).

Each and every passage above could launch a series of sermons unpacking the importance and significance of God's Word. But it is sufficient to say that when believers gather to study and share insights from the Scriptures, they are encouraging and blessing one another just as the whole colony of bees benefits from the honey-making process. When studied and handled properly, the Scriptures are invaluable to those who hear it. But if Scripture is not used properly it can be harmful (legalism) or spiritually lethal (cults). Misapplied Scripture is harmful, or at least useless, just as fermented honey is of no use to the bees.

Just as honey is an antiseptic to cure bodily infections, the Scriptures are a salve to the soul. By following the Scriptures in daily life, one can avoid many heartaches and pain. The Bible contains guidelines regarding morality, relationships, finances, health, marriage, family, work and mental well-being to name a few. Just watch the evening news and assess how much needless pain and suffering could be avoided in the world if the guidance of God's Word was being implemented. What would be on the news if there were no murders, rapes, robberies, bribes, lying, cheating, corruption, extortion, abuse, neglect, hatred, selfishness, pride, anger, jealous, racism, drug use. . . ?

Would you eat just one meal a week every week? Probably not. Yet many believers who do not read their Bibles are relying upon the Sunday sermon to feed their souls. Needless to say, this is not healthy. Yet this seems to be prevalent within the church. In fact, a large parachurch group recognized a high degree of biblical illiteracy among its staff. Why are believers not reading the Scriptures? The reasons vary from person to person. Some would claim they are too busy with family or career. Some would probably state the Bible is too difficult for the average layman to understand so why bother. Others may not read it because they are afraid of the truth especially with Hebrews 4:12 in mind: "For the word of God is living and active and sharper than any two-edged sword, and piercing as far as the division of soul and spirit, of both joints and marrow, and able to judge the thoughts and intentions of the heart."

Too busy? Granted there may be seasons in our lives that are very demanding, but a constant state of busy-ness may be an indication of misplaced or missing priorities. As difficult as it may seem, take some time to reflect on how you spend your time and see if it matches your priorities.

Too difficult? Welcome to the club. Every believer, at one time or another, struggles with parts of the Bible, including seminary graduates. For starters, try reading Eugene Peterson's *The Message* which is a very readable and down-to-earth version of the Bible. Next, try using a study Bible and refer to the notes, maps and other explanations it contains. When studying specific passages, take advantage of commentaries which can be very helpful in providing further explanation and insight. The important thing to remember is not to give up—studying the Bible is a lifetime quest. The more you read and study, the clearer the Bible will become.

Afraid? Your honesty is admirable, but I cannot help you. Dealing with God is very serious. Nothing is hidden from the omniscient One. God gives us His Word to shine light into the darkened corners of our hearts. Once a problem is revealed, one can choose to conform to His will or not. One can read the Bible like any other textbook for intellectual purposes. In this case, only the mind is affected. If you read the

Bible realizing it is God's Word, then be prepared to confront its truths with all of the associated ramifications it will have on your life.

Just as honey does not go bad, neither does God's Word. Its messages are timeless and have been revealed by a loving God through His prophets or apostles and recorded for us. Has your Bible been collecting dust? Blow off the dust, pick it up and dig in. The awkwardness will pass, and the words will start to flow as you spend more time with it just as crystallized honey will start to flow when it is warmed. God is faithful. He will never leave us or forsake us despite our wandering hearts and minds. When He draws us back to himself, it is usually through the message of His Word.

So pick up your Bible, dig in and Bon Appetite!

A word about the Word

The accuracy and reliability of the Bible is constantly being attacked and challenged. For example, during the writing of this book the discovery of the "Gospel of Judas" was announced. Some will use this to raise questions about how the New Testament text was chosen. How does a believer respond to such arguments?

Starting with the Old Testament, a firm case for the accuracy and reliability of Old Testament text was established by the discovery and study of the Dead Sea Scrolls. These scrolls contained all, or portions of all, of the Old Testament books except for Esther. Also, the Jewish first-century historian

Josephus recorded a collection of the Old Testament books that matches our current list. Furthermore, Jesus Himself put His stamp of approval upon the entire Old Testament Scriptures in Matthew 23:35. In that verse He referred to the murders of Abel and Zechariah. Why are these two people significant? Abel is mentioned in Genesis, and Zechariah is in 2 Chronicles. Unlike our Old Testament which goes from Genesis to Malachi, the Hebrew Bible goes from Genesis to Second Chronicles, but it contains all of the books that are in our Old Testament.[12]

With the Old Testament being a closed group of writings (that is, once finalized no more writings were to be included), it is reasonable to assume the New Testament writings would also be a fixed collection. Just as God used prophets in the Old Testament, He used the apostles in the New Testament. When the apostolic age ended, so also ended the time for other writings to be considered as candidates for inclusion in the New Testament. Thus, for this reason as well as others, the "Gospel of Judas" would be excluded as it is a second century writing.

As for the New Testament contents a wealth of supporting information has survived through the centuries. For example, there are over five thousand Greek manuscripts, in a variety of formats, which contain various portions of the New Testament. If one also counts the manuscripts written in other languages, such as Latin, Ethiopic, Slavic and Armenian, the total is about twenty-four thousand. Aside from these manuscripts there are important supporting records from the first-century Jewish historian Josephus and

Roman sources from the early second century, such as Tacitus and Pliny the Younger.[13] In short, no other document from antiquity has such attestation as does the New Testament.

Regarding the selection of the contents of the New Testament, several important criteria were used. Authorship was very important as the New Testament books were written by apostles (for example, Matthew, John and Paul) or associates of the apostles. (Mark was an associate of Peter, and Luke traveled with Paul). No one is completely certain who wrote the wonderful book of Hebrews (guesses include Paul, Luke and Apollos), but the writing of this book can be dated to before 70 A.D., and thus content and age are other criteria. Another criterion is that the contents of the writing were in agreement with the messages contained in the undoubted apostolic writings. The early churches circulated letters and documents as seen in Colossians 4:16 when the Colossians were told to swap letters with the Laodiceans, and James circulated letters concerning the Jerusalem Council decision in Acts 15. Therefore, because of the circulation of these early documents, it is reasonable to conclude the early churches had a good collection of the apostolic writings. Thus, another criterion was that the writings were well known among the churches. For a more thorough explanation of how the New Testament texts came to be included in the Bible, check out *The Canon of Scripture* by F. F. Bruce.[14]

Were the writers of the New Testament text conscious they were to write Scripture in addition to the Old Testament? We do not have the answer to this, but we know they did recognize some of their writings as Scripture at an early date (~ 63–67 A.D.). For instance, Paul quotes Luke 10:7 and refers to it as Scripture in 1 Timothy 5:18. Also, in 2 Peter 3:16, Peter refers to a collection of Paul's writings as Scripture.

Were the apostles concerned about the accuracy of their writing? Paul certainly was. He issued a statement in 2 Thessalonians 2:2 regarding a fake message and used his signature at the end of the epistle as a seal of authenticity. Thus, the precedent had been set for the early church to be on guard for and protect against false writings.

This was just a brief overview of the accuracy and reliability of the Scriptures and is by no means complete. The bottom line is there is reasonable evidence to conclude that the Scriptures we have today are accurate and reliable.

Chapter 14

Winter of the Soul

~⋅~

Bees don't hibernate. They huddle.

During the warm months the members of the colony work feverishly, hence the phrase "busy as a bee." While the lazy drones just hang out, countless chores are done by tens of thousands of worker bees. Cleaning, nursery care, scouting, gathering pollen, collecting nectar, ripening honey, guarding the hive, tending to the queen, making wax, building comb, capping honey, ventilation. Then winter comes. The activity nearly comes to a complete stop. Once the drones have been evicted and cold weather closes in, the members of the colony cluster together to form a ball inside the hive. The hollow warm interior of this ball is where the winter brood is incubated.

While in this cluster the bees will rotate from the interior of this huddle to the exterior and then work their way back in. This process continues so that no bee will spend too much time on the exterior and freeze to death as most of the inside of the hive is about the same temperature as the outside air. While part of this cluster, some bees may crawl into a cell to fill what would otherwise be a void in the formation. This cluster will shrink and expand in response to the temperature outside the hive. The colder the temperature, the smaller and tighter the cluster will be to keep warm. As the temperature moderates, the cluster will expand since not as much warmth is needed.[1] By contracting and expanding the cluster, the bees regulate the temperature at the center of the cluster where the queen and brood are located.

I try not to bother my bees too much either in the winter or the warmer months. But it is necessary occasionally to take a quick peak inside during the winter to monitor their food supply. The cluster of bees will work its way upward as the winter progresses. The cluster must remain in contact with honey in order to feed itself. Therefore there always needs to be honey directly above the cluster. Bees are reluctant to break the cluster during the winter. Many a colony has starved to death even though there were full frames of honey on either side of the cluster. On a few occasions when I noticed there was not much honey above the cluster in my hive, I made "bee candy" (a hard sugar mixture) and placed it directly above the bees to ensure something was there for them to eat as they worked their way upward.

The winter period is crucial for the bees. Obviously, the survival of the colony is at stake. If they survive, the strength of the colony going into the spring will determine how successful it will be as a honey producer in the coming summer. With a strong colony emerging from the winter, the bees will be able to gather more pollen from the early blooming plants. This abundance of pollen will in turn prompt the queen to lay more eggs. With more eggs come more bees. By having the population peak at the proper time, the colony will be able to take full advantage of the major nectar-producing plants in early summer. Honey made from this source of nectar will be the bulk of the food which is stored for the coming winter. A colony that is weak coming into the spring will probably struggle throughout the year and may not produce any extra honey. A colony that does not survive the winter leaves the beekeeper with a void that will have to be filled with a replacement colony. This replacement colony will most likely start out with a small population and probably will not produce a honey crop either until the following year.

Several key factors determine the likelihood that a colony will successfully survive the winter. First, and obviously, there needs to be sufficient food stores within the hive. Next, the hive must have a good queen. A good queen will be a good egg producer. As stated above, with more eggs come more bees. The greater the number of bees going into the winter, the better the colony will be able to cluster together and keep warm. Third, the beekeeper may wrap the hive with an insulating material to help conserve heat. If the hive temperature drops, the bees will have to eat more of their supplies to generate the necessary heat. The more the bees eat, the greater the probability that they will exhaust their supplies and starve to death before spring arrives with fresh sources of food. Fourth, sheltering the hive behind a wind break will minimize the impact of cold winter winds and thus will help the bees conserve food.

Lastly, the hive will need a top entrance. Each hive has a standard entrance at the bottom. This entrance will be greatly reduced by beekeepers to minimize cold air from entering the hive and to keep rodents out. The entrance cannot be completely sealed shut because the bees need to be able to breathe and to leave for cleansing flights on mild winter days. As older bees die during the winter, they fall from the cluster and collect on the bottom of the hive. If there is not a small top entrance, the accumulation of dead bees could prevent air from entering the bottom entrance and the colony could suffocate. This top entrance also allows water vapor to escape. The water vapor is a byproduct of the bees as they generate heat. The vapor needs to escape so it will not condense and accumulate in the hive. Moisture collecting within the hive can severely challenge the bees' ability to remain warm. If the challenge is too great, the developing brood will become chilled and die as well as the adult bees.[2]

Just as honeybees must deal with winter, so also do God's people face winter seasons of the soul. These are times when God seems distant. The joy of our salvation has long since faded. Our prayers do not seem to make it past the ceiling. We often feel lonely or isolated from what God is doing around us. The Scriptures do not speak to our hearts as they once did before. All areas of life become drudgery. In short, it is a time of testing of our faith. We wonder if God is real and start to think our relationship with

Him is akin to that of a child with an imaginary invisible friend.

Sometimes we are the cause of these winters whereas some winters "just happen." My Christian life has been punctuated by several of these winters. They were of varying lengths and severity. There were times that seemed to sneak up on me, and then I would suddenly realize the "abundant life" did not seem very abundant. A severe winter struck while I was actively involved in a campus ministry in college. I had just come off a summer mission's project in which God had miraculously raised the necessary funding for me to go. I was in a discipleship group as well as leading one. When I should have been pumped, I was completely deflated spiritually. Darkness and hopelessness set in. Life at that time truly did not seem worth the effort.

In hindsight that winter was largely self-induced because I was focusing on what I was *doing* instead of resting in *being* God's child. One of the constant struggles in my life has involved *doing* versus *being*. I would wrongly consider my service to God and my relationship with Him to be one and the same. It would seem reasonable to me that if I was involved with ministry activities I must be close with God. In reality it is too easy to get caught up in doing Christian activities while leaving Christ out of it. I need to remind myself that my relationship with God is distinct from my service to God. Although faith and works go hand-in-hand (James 2:14-26), one's service to God should always stem from one's relationship with God. This is seen in Paul's statement that the only thing that matters is "faith working through love" (Galatians 5:6) and in John's admonition that "whoever keeps His word, in him the love of God has truly been perfected" (1 John 2:5). During that winter my service to and relationship with God were somehow combined or confused, and the service eventually drained the life out of me.

The Bible points out that many heroes of the faith had their unique winters as well when God seemed distant. Abraham waited years for the fulfilled promise of an heir. Joseph undeservedly spent considerable time in prison before being promoted to pharaoh's right-hand man. Moses was tending sheep for forty years before a burning bush lit a fire under him. In the early days of Samuel, when Eli was the prophet, a word from the Lord was rare. Job's life fell apart in an instant. David spent several years fleeing for his life after being anointed king. At one point Elijah thought he was the last prophet until God told him otherwise. Jonah spent three days (that would have seemed like an eternity) inside a great fish. Nehemiah prayed for about four months before God moved the king's heart to permit the walls of Jerusalem to be rebuilt. Jeremiah was thrown into a dungeon. Hosea was directed to marry an unfaithful wife. The Jewish people endured more than four centuries of silence after Malachi's ink dried. Jesus was alone in the wilderness for forty days before starting His ministry. Paul, after a long and successful missionary career, was in a cold prison awaiting execution. John was exiled to Patmos by Rome because of his faith. From Genesis to Revelation God's people hit low points. They were caused by different reasons, under different circumstances, and were of various durations and degrees of severity. No one is immune. For those who subscribe to a "health, wealth and prosperity gospel," I simply suggest you read the Bible—the whole Bible.

Given that winters of the soul are inevitable, what lessons can be learned from the bees?

First, one must have an adequate supply of food. As mentioned in the previous chapter, God's Word was likened to honey. The sincere follower of Christ will be a reader of the Bible. It contains God's truths which are displayed in numerous settings involving many flawed individuals like us. If you are ignorant of the Scriptures, you are depriving yourself of a vital source of encouragement and comfort when winter comes. Reading the Bible is probably the last thing a struggling Christian wants to do. If you immersed yourself in it during your soul's summer, though, you at least will have a recollection of key passages to cling to when your winter comes.

Second, hang out with your brothers and sisters in Christ. When you are down, huddling with others may not seem to be a desirable thing to do either. But within the cluster of other believers "one anothering" can take place in a warm and loving environment. Be willing to share your struggles. Of course, there will be those who, with good intentions, will offer words of advice or some Scripture passages that will sound like clichés. But it's guaranteed someone can relate and share their experience. That person, or persons, will be a light in your dark cold winter that will help you to endure and continue onward.

Third, insulate yourself from the source of your struggle. Identify the crux of your problem and avoid situations or people that aggravate the problem. For example, if you are struggling with the reliability of Scripture, then do not read books that undermine the Scriptures. If materialism is getting the best of you, stay out of fancy department stores and do not drive through high-priced housing developments. If God seems to be a million miles away, it might be a good idea to distance yourself from those bubbly believers who are always talking about God's presence in their lives. Although you do not want to insulate yourself entirely from God's people, some instances and personalities can be especially annoying when you are struggling. But temporarily putting some space between you and your irritations can be a start on the road to recovery. When you are past the low point of your struggle and your spirit is stronger, then you will be in a much better position to tackle the things that get the best of you. Through Christ we are more than conquerors (Romans 8:37). We should never surrender to anyone or anything. But a strategic temporary retreat may be necessary at times.

Fourth, get out of the weather. If you are in a winter season, it may be best to get out of the whirlwind of life's, or ministry's, hustle and bustle. Busy-ness can zap the life out of us, drain us of our endurance and then leave us starving mentally, emotionally and spiritually. A wise person knows when to get out of the race, or at least to slow down, and try to rest for a while. A classic depiction of this is the scene when Jesus visits Martha and Mary.

> Now as they were traveling along, He entered a village; and a woman named Martha welcomed Him into her home. She had a sister called Mary, who was seated at the Lord's feet, listening to His word. But Martha was distracted with all her preparations; and she came up to Him and said, "Lord, do You not care that my sister has left me to do all the serving alone? Then tell her to help me." But the Lord answered and said to her, "Martha, Martha, you are worried and bothered about so many things; but only one thing is necessary, for Mary has chosen the good part, which shall not be taken away from her" (Luke 10:38-42).

Martha was frantically scurrying about the kitchen attempting to serve Jesus while Mary was quietly seated at His feet enjoying His presence. We are not told exactly what the "one thing" is; but it is obvious Martha was too busy, and it was getting the best of her. Every one is busy; but if you are too busy like Martha to spend time with Jesus and others, then you are too busy. Another negative example Martha displays is that weary people start to point fingers at others when they cannot meet their own standards.

Last, do not let your burden suffocate you. Do not sit around and stew in your own juices for too long. Some introspective reflection is good, but too much can be paralyzing. Get away for a breath of fresh air. Get out for a change of scenery. Treat yourself to a weekend away to a favorite spot where you can reflect on what is going on in your life. Seek God's wise counsel and let Him fill your longing heart. Sometimes God uses church retreats or conferences to speak to us in just the right way. Also, ask friends for their recommendations regarding helpful books to read and ponder. Ecclesiastes tells us there is nothing new under the sun. This means your struggle is not unique. Someone else has been through it before you and has written about it. Learn from their observations and insights.

How well we emerge from our winter season will affect our future. If we are severely weakened, it will take longer to recover. If your winter does not seem to end, then by all means seek professional help. Your problem could be deep rooted and therefore need special attention.

It is hoped we will emerge stronger for going through a winter season. Consider what James says: "Consider it all joy, my brethren, when you encounter various trials, knowing that the testing of your faith produces endurance. And let endurance have its perfect result, so that you may be perfect and complete, lacking in nothing" (James 1:2-4). God uses our trials for our betterment. In this passage the benefit of trials is endurance which in turn leads to perfecting and completeness so that we will not lack anything. None of us wants to be lacking in anything in regard to our faith. But the key to this is endurance. Endurance is exactly the character trait we need when our winter season drags on. "When will this end?" we ask ourselves as we silently wonder if we are going to make it through.

During these times we will usually ask ourselves and God, "What is going on?" or "Why does my spiritual life feel so cold?" I find it interesting that the next verse in James is a directive to ask for wisdom. "But if any of you lacks wisdom, let him ask of God, who gives to all generously and without reproach, and it will be given to him" (James 1:5). This is a very popular verse and was probably one of the first Bible verses I ever memorized. I have heard it quoted often in Christian circles as people offer it as advice to others who are seeking answers to life's general questions. Although it is not incorrect to ask God for wisdom as we go through life, the context of James 1:5 is specifically to seek God's wisdom in times of trial. During the long winter days we should be doing some soul searching. We need to ask ourselves and God tough questions. "Why am I going through this? What are You trying to teach me? What false idols do I have in my life? What do You want me to learn about You? What needs to change in my heart?" Ask God for wisdom to discern the answers to these questions.

Maturing as a Christian comes not solely through studying the Scriptures. Most lessons learned well come from the wise application of Scripture to life's situations. Ask God for His wisdom when your soul is in winter. Be patient and practice endurance. Wait for God's gentle word of revelation and take it to heart. He is faithful. "For I am confident of this very thing, that He who began a good work in you will perfect it until the day of Christ Jesus" (Philippians 1:6).

Just as a colony of bees that has successfully survived the winter will be better prepared for the coming summer season, so also Christians that emerge from a soul-winter can be better prepared for God's service. Sometimes God does His best work in us during the winter.

Chapter 15

Mutiny

Occasionally, when a colony has experienced a traumatic event, such as when the hive has incurred significant damage, the bees will "ball the queen." For unknown reasons the entire colony will attack the queen, cling to her and form a tightly packed ball. This ball will be so dense the queen is either crushed to death or suffocated.

There are several instances in which "balling" may occur. If a hive is toppled over in an act of vandalism, the bees can turn upon their queen.[1] Frequent intrusions into the hive by beekeepers can also prompt balling.[2] Another reason the workers may ball the queen is to eliminate an old failing queen to make way for a new one they have raised. Also, sometimes when beekeepers improperly insert a new queen into a hive, the workers will reject her and ball her to death.[3]

From a human standpoint this behavior of the worker bees seems counter intuitive. Since bees are generally good communicators, one would think that in the face of harsh adversity the bees would regroup by rallying around the queen. She is, after all, the center of attention and plays a vital role in populating the hive and in maintaining social order by means of her pheromones. As goes the queen, so goes the rest of the colony. So why this collegial act of mindless vengeance upon the most important member of the colony? We may never know. Perhaps if the bees had a better understanding of what was happening to their hive, then they would be more inclined to work together rather than take out their confusion and anger on the queen.

Churches can behave similarly. When a problem arises, who normally bears the brunt of the congregation's wrath? The pastor. If he's lucky (or smart), the entire leadership team will be taken to task and not just the pastor.

One large church I had attended experienced a major uprising by the members. The problem, which was never fully resolved, came to light just before the election and installation of a new elder board. Once word of a "problem" got out, however, the congregation came in mass to various meetings armed with their perspectives or opinions of what happened or what should be done. Then the election occurred. Previous elections were uneventful as the members were rather indifferent to the running of the church government as all of the positions were filled. In this instance, though, due to the election criteria and the way the votes were cast, only a handful of the approximately two dozen positions were filled. In essence, the congregation "balled" the leadership of the church. At this point with everyone involved, laity and leaders alike, things were hopelessly awry, and all hope of unity was lost. To make a long story short, a split eventually took place between the elders and the pastoral staff. The church membership split three ways—some sided with the elders and some with the pastoral staff, and the rest simply left in disgust to go elsewhere.

Because of the size and renown of this church, this problem was known literally around the world. Sadly, instead of coming together to reconcile and regroup, the once peaceful and prosperous church was torn apart. The reputations of the church, pastors and elders were now stained. Relationships were strained or shattered. There was no going back to the way things once were.

There are a few lessons to be learned here. First, the leaders of the church must communicate among one another to be able to identify and address issues in their early stages. In the above situation not everyone in leadership at this church was aware of the original issue. Second, the leadership needs to communicate with the congregation regarding changes within the church or of any significant issues. (If the leaders do not keep each other informed, then do not expect the congregation to have an accurate picture of what is going on either.) Finally, every member of a church needs to be informed so they can pray intelligently for their leaders and the important issues facing their church.

There is another point to make about bees. Although the queen bee is the most important individual member of a colony, she may not be in charge.

We should not automatically assume she calls all the shots simply because the title "queen" is most often associated with monarchies or rulers of countries. Some believe several "control bees" direct the activities of the colony such as swarming, the amount and timing of egg laying done by the queen, and the ejection of the drones in the fall.

But regarding godly leadership it appears a plurality of elders existed at each church mentioned in the New Testament. Pastor-run churches are common among today's nondenominational movements. But there is no clear biblical example to support such a leadership model. Although no standard form of church government is set forth in the Bible, it appears that elders (plural) shouldered the lion's share of the leadership duties. Why make this point? In addition to following the biblical notion of a leadership team, it is more difficult to "ball" several leaders rather than just one.

One could arguably make the case that the pastor is the most important person in the church because of the many things he does (administrate, counsel and teach) and because of his high visibility on Sunday mornings. Accountability, the prayerful application of checks and balances, as well as delegation of responsibility and authority among church members and leaders can be beneficial, though. It could go a long way in preventing pastor burnout, sustaining the mission of the church, maximizing human resources and developing future leaders.

Absolute power corrupts absolutely. There should be no such thing as a "benevolent dictator" running any church no matter how sincere or dedicated the pastor or head elder may be. Jesus did not come to be served but to serve (Matthew 20:28). When we read the New Testament passages about the disciples arguing among themselves about who was the greatest, we all shake our heads in disbelief that they were so clueless about Jesus' message and example. Yet power struggles exist today and have been common in the church down through history.

Servant leadership was advocated by Jesus, not self-promotion. When was the last time you witnessed a foot washing (John 13:1-20)? It is uncertain who would be more humbled — the washer or the one being washed. Leaders are to lead by humble example, not from a position of authority. Furthermore, unity in love should be present within a body of believers (Ephesians 4:1-3). This especially includes unity among church leaders to be living examples to their flocks (1 Peter 5:3).

Perhaps if the bees could communicate more clearly among themselves about their situation, then they might not be inclined to ball the queen bee so quickly. Perhaps if churches communicated better, then issues could be identified and addressed quickly and properly by the leadership and thus avoid an unnecessary uprising from the congregation. Why should a mutiny or a self-destructive implosion occur within a church? Perhaps this is one behavior we should not copy from the bees.

Chapter 16

Smoke

You have probably seen pictures or videos of beekeepers entering a hive and using a can-shaped object that makes smoke. In case you were wondering, that object is called a smoker. It is a combustion chamber that is connected to a bellows. The chamber holds some kind of slow-burning material while the bellows blows air into it to fan the smoldering material and thus generates smoke. (See Figure 2 for a sketch of a smoker.)

Beekeepers will puff the smoke into the hive before they open it. They will also periodically puff smoke on the bees while they are working in the hive. The smoke has two basic effects upon the bees. One, it blocks the honeybees' receptors and overwhelms the alarm scent of the guard bees and thus inhibits the bees' ability to communicate. Blocking this scent prevents the entire colony from being called to battle stations. This will result in the bees being in a state of confusion and thus make things easier for the beekeeper. Second, the smoke causes the bees to stuff themselves with honey. The thinking behind this might be that the smoke causes the bees to believe the hive is on fire and they will have to evacuate. Therefore, before abandoning the hive, the bees would try to take as much honey with them as possible.

Eating all of this honey has two benefits for the beekeeper. First, if the bees are busy eating honey, then they are not readily available to attack the beekeeper. Second, when the bees fill themselves with honey, they are then physically incapable of stinging. In order to sting, the bees must bend their bodies with the stinger pointed toward the target. When the bees are full of honey, they cannot bend their bodies and thus cannot sting. As an analogy recall how difficult it is to bend over and untie your shoes after eating a large holiday meal. Typically the most comfortable position after such a meal is to lie down flat on your back. Being full of honey and unable to sting, the bees will usually remain relatively calm.

If one does not smoke the bees prior to entering the hive, one is asking for trouble. I learned this lesson firsthand as a teenager while assisting my father. A few days after extracting a super full of honey, my father directed me to place the empty super back on the hive from which it came. He wanted me to put it under the topmost super of the hive. So I donned my protective gear, picked up the super and headed toward the hive. I had briefly entertained the thought of using our smoker but had convinced myself it would literally take only about twenty seconds to accomplish my assigned task and therefore it was not necessary or worth the effort to fire up the smoker.

Bee Parables

When I got to the hive I mentally rehearsed my actions to place the empty super back on the hive. I would lift off the top cover, remove the inner cover, lift off up the topmost super and set it to the side of the hive; put the empty super in place, pick up the topmost super and put it on top of the empty super; put the inner cover on top of it and finish the task by capping things off with the top cover. "No big deal," I thought to myself. Teenagers do have a tendency to be overly optimistic while wrongly believing in their invincibility.

When I went to lift the top cover it would not move. The bees had glued it in place. I was aware the bees glue hive components together, but I did not think they would have had a chance to do so since we had taken the hive apart only a few days earlier. So to remove the top cover I needed to hit it with the heel of my palm to dislodge it from the bee glue. It took several strikes of my hand to break it free. But with each strike of my hand I agitated the bees more and more as their collective humming from inside of the hive grew louder and louder.

I also found that the flat inner cover was glued securely in place. I had to use the top cover as a hammer to hit the inner cover and knock it free. By now the bees were more than a little ticked off, and dozens of bees were flying about me to let me know good things were not about to happen if I did not gracefully retreat. I understood their reaction but decided to continue since all that remained to do was to lift off the top super.

Some of us are slow learners. Even though the top cover and inner cover were glued securely in place, I thought I could easily lift off the top super because the side handles would provide me with a good grip and I could gently remove the top super. Wrong! When I went to lift the top super I had positioned myself in such a way that my arms and legs were set to lift the super straight up. In this position my face was a few inches directly above a super full of bees. I remember staring down at the bees and recalling being this close to them during previous inspections. When staring into a hive, it always amazed and fascinated me that so many bees could fit into the small spaces between the frames.

As I went to lift the super, as a weightlifter would attempt to pick up a heavy load, I let out a breath of air from my lungs when the super did not budge. If it was not my bad breath, then it was the simple fact that the bees, already being upset, instantly realized I did not belong there so they literally jumped into action. Before I realized what had happened, hundreds of bees simultaneously came out of the super and covered my veil like a magnet picking up metal shavings. So thick were the bees on my veil that I could not see a thing! I had never experienced anything remotely similar to this reaction from the bees in the past. Instinctively I shook my head to clear the bees from my veil. As panic came over me, my adrenaline kicked in. I ripped off the top super. More bees came pouring out of the hive. I was literally covered with bees as I frantically put the empty super in place and reassembled the hive and left the area.

But the bees were not finished with me. After a beekeeper leaves a hive a few bees hover around him to escort him from the area. These escorts usually return to the hive after the beekeeper is several feet away from the hive. After quickly moving several yards away from the hive I was still covered in bees, and more were circling me. I shook myself and brushed myself off with my gloved hands to try to rid myself of the bees. Some left but not many. As I continued walking away from the hive, the bees were still pursuing me in hot displeasure.

Not having a smoker, I could not hide my scent or the scent of dozens of stingers in my clothing that were acting as homing beacons for the bees. It was as if I had been targeted and bees were locked on like radar. I could not go into the house because dozens, if not hundreds, of bees would have come in with me and attacked my family members. (Who says teenagers are not considerate?) To escape my tormentors I had to run. I zigged and zagged while darting under low-hanging branches and through bushes. I was thankful we lived out in the country, and no one was around watching. (My teenage pride was spared.) If anyone would have seen me they might have thought I was losing my mind because I ran like a wild animal. I do not remember how long or far I had to run, but eventually the bees left me to return to the hive. When I realized they were gone, I collapsed to the ground to catch my breath. While lying there on my back panting like a dog and staring up to the sky, I rationalized (as only a teenager can) that I really did not need a smoker after all.

Today, if I could improve one part of my beekeeping effort it would have to be in the operation of my smoker. I cannot always find the right combination of material to burn. The combustible material needs to be easy to ignite, burn slowly and make a lot of smoke. If I do get the right combination that makes a good supply of smoke, I usually then forget to pump the bellows periodically to feed oxygen into the can to sustain the combustion. I have talked with other beekeepers who have expressed similar complaints. Some have experimented with different mixtures of combustibles (corn cobs, old pine needles, dried grass clippings, wood chips, rags and even chewing tobacco). Some have had more success when they bought a different model smoker and claimed that not all smokers are created equal. But for a beekeeper a smoker that generates a lot of smoke for a long time is an absolute essential when working in the hive to calm the bees and jam their communications.

The equivalent to smoke in a Christian's life is sin. What is sin? Simply, it is anything—thought, word, attitude, action or inaction—that is contrary to God's perfect character.[1] Although sin does not destroy a believer's standing with God, it impedes his or her ability to communicate and fellowship with Him. King David wrote, "If I regard wickedness in my heart, the Lord will not hear" (Psalm 66:18). Peter echoed something similar in 1 Peter 3:7 when he wrote about a husband's prayer life being affected if he is not treating his wife properly. Not only does sin affect the individual, it can also have a corporate effect as indicated in 2 Chronicles 7:14—"and My people who are called by My name humble themselves and pray and seek My face and turn from their wicked ways, then I will hear from heaven, will forgive their sin and will heal their land."

Why do we sin? Even as a Christian with a new heart from God (Jeremiah 32:39), we are still afflicted by the remnants of our old sinful and wayward nature. We can very easily be attracted to something that is contrary to God's will for us. Even the apostle Paul describes his struggle with sin in Romans 7:15-25 where he admitted to doing things he should not do and not doing things he should. The author of Hebrews makes an accurate assessment of the human plight with the statement about "the passing pleasures of sin" (11:25). In other words, if sin did not have some appeal to it, we would not be interested in it. Thus, our old nature coupled with alluring enticements results in yielding to the temptations of sin.

There are sins of commission (action) and sins of omission (inaction). Most people are familiar with sins resulting from inappropriate actions. But sins of omission must not be ignored. Sitting on the sideline of life is easy to do especially when one sees the trials of other Christians who are actively living their faith. The apostle James, who wrote his epistle to prompt believers to live out their faith, says, "Therefore, to one who knows the right thing to do and does not do it, to him it is sin"(James 4:17). Passivity is no excuse. If you know what God is directing you to do, then do it. Just because no one else knows what God is laying upon your heart, it does not mean you will not be held responsible.

The effects of sin are many. Sin can inhibit a lifestyle of faith or trust (Romans 14:23). Sexual sins can harm the physical body (1 Corinthians 6:18). Sin can cause one's heart to be hardened (Hebrews 3:13). Sin encumbers and entangles believers in their living out the Christian faith (Hebrews 12:1). The apostle John even wrote of sin leading to physical death (1 John 5:16). Whether major or minor, either immediately or delayed, the consequences of sin will impact us.

When smoke causes bees to stuff themselves with food, it is likened to Christians overindulging themselves in one thing or another that inhibits them from doing the things they should. Consider the sin of worldliness—loving the things of this world more than God—that had quite an impact upon James's audience in their relationships to each other and to God. "What is the source of quarrels and conflicts among you? Is not the source your pleasures that wage war in your members? You lust and do not have; so you commit murder. You are envious and cannot obtain; so you fight and quarrel. You do not have because you do not ask. You ask and do not receive, because you ask with wrong motives, so that you may spend it on your pleasures. You adulteresses, do you not know that friendship with the world is hostility toward God? Therefore whoever wishes to be a friend of the world makes himself an enemy of God" (James 4:1-4).

After James had scolded his audience, he reminded them of God's goodness. "Or do you think that the Scripture speaks to no purpose: 'He jealously desires the Spirit which He has made to dwell in us'? But He gives a greater grace" (James 4:5-6). Some Bible translations render this last sentence as "He gives us more grace." The implication is that the grace of God will always be greater than our sins. Even though we know better and we are sorely disappointed with ourselves because of our inclination to sin, God is always there patiently waiting for us to come back to Him.

Jesus illustrated the endless love and grace of God in the story of the prodigal son (Luke 15:11-32). After the son left home he depleted his share of his father's inheritance on wild living. He was broke and had fallen on tough times, and his thoughts turned toward home. He prepared a speech of confession and contrition for his father and headed for home. Evidently the father had been scanning the horizon since the day his son left in hopes of seeing him again. When the son was returning home, the father spotted him at a distance and ran to him. When they met, the son's speech was delayed because he was embraced by his father who smothered him with kisses. The father did not need to hear the speech before pouring out his love on his son. He was overjoyed that his son had returned. In this story God is the father, and we all are the prodigal. We, as His children, can do nothing to earn, or alter, the special place we have in God's heart. When we sin we should be remorseful but not to the point of wallowing in guilt or self-deprecation. Take heart—God loves us as we are more than we will ever know. May we never grow tired of the story of the prodigal son.

It is of great comfort to know God is there for us when we fall, but we still need to be mindful of the awful effects sin has on our personal lives, as mentioned above, and also within the church. Keep a close personal walk with God. Do not let unconfessed sin accumulate in your life. If we confess our sins, He will forgive us (1 John 1:9). If we maintain a right relationship with God, it will help in our relationships with others. The evil one would like to use our weaknesses and failures to divide the church and thwart the advancement of God's kingdom. Do not play into his hand. Be quick to right any wrongs you might have committed against another person. Whatever you do, do it with love. "Above all, keep fervent in your love for one another, because love covers a multitude of sins" (1 Peter 4:8). If someone has wronged you, be willing to forgive. We always need to be mindful to "be kind to one another, tenderhearted, forgiving each other, just as God in Christ also has forgiven you" (Ephesians 4:32).

Just as smoke causes the individual bees to overindulge in consuming food when they should be defending the hive, so also can sin in the life of a believer divert him or her when they should be doing God's will. Also, just as smoke renders the entire colony of bees into a hapless state of confusion and impedes their ability to work together, likewise the unity of a church is disrupted when sin is allowed to fester among its members. Do not let sin on a personal or an interpersonal level interfere with God's plan for your life or the ministry of your church.

Figure 2: A Smoker
(Courtesy of Brushy Mountain Bee Farm Inc.)

Chapter 17

Stuck on You

One of the lesser known bee products is propolis. Propolis, also called "bee glue," is a sticky resin or gum the bees typically collect from poplar or pine trees.[1] It is an important item for the health and well being of the colony. Bees have several uses for propolis. It is used to seal cracks in the hive or fill gaps between the supers to keep out small insect pests and cold winter winds. The bees also like to glue the frames securely to the supers. Basically, anywhere there is a gap or crack created where things join together, the bees will fill it with propolis. In the wild the bees use it to line the interior surface of their home such as a hollow cavity in a tree. This lining will act as an antiseptic to kill most unwanted bacteria within the hive, and it can protect the tree cavity from further decay.[2]

Beekeepers hate propolis. Many beekeepers have damaged frames during hive inspections because of bee glue. To properly inspect the hive a beekeeper needs to withdraw and examine the frames. Because of the bonding strength of the propolis the beekeeper needs to apply considerable force to free the frames. If the force necessary to free the frame is greater than the strength of the frame's wooden parts, the frame will break. If the frame breaks, it will need to be removed from the hive and replaced. Making the comb on a new frame will cost the bees time and effort and will have some impact upon the beekeeper's honey crop.

Because of propolis beekeepers will use special tools which are indispensable. The hive tool, which is a mini-crow bar with sharp flat edges, is used to break the seal between the supers and to pry the individual frames loose. Once the frames have been loosened, a frame gripper is attached to the top of the frame. The frame gripper is basically a double set of pliers. Once attached to the frame, the beekeeper can apply an even force to pull the frame completely free from the propolis. (See Figure 3 for a sketch of a hive tool and frame gripper.)

In addition to the potential problems that propolis presents to beekeepers when removing frames, it is just plain annoying. It has the tackiness of an oil-based paint or pine sap. If you have ever touched this type of wet paint or sap, you will recall that it is very sticky and will not wash off with regular soap and water. Unless you use some kind of solvent, the paint and sap will stay on your skin and remain sticky until it literally wears off. Propolis has the identical characteristics. Beekeepers cannot avoid this stuff while working in a hive. Therefore, they will get this glue directly on their hands or their gloves. Either way it makes it difficult to handle equipment and hive components. Fingers will not move freely as they stick together. Sometimes it is difficult to release tools to set them down as they may remain stuck to one's hands or gloves.

I have experienced this frustration when attempting to set down my hive tool to free my hand. When I thought I was letting go of the tool, it was actually partially stuck to my glove. (The fact that my sense of touch was compromised by wearing the glove did not help matters either.) So after I thought I had released the tool to lay it on the top of a super I moved my hand to reach for my smoker. When I moved my hand with the tool partially stuck to my glove, the tool came along for the ride. Of course, it did not remain stuck to my glove. It detached itself from my glove and was flung in the direction in which I had moved my hand. Naturally it landed on the ground just beyond my reach. Since I knew I would need the tool shortly, I had to pick it up. Therefore I had to break the rhythm of what I was doing to pick up the tool. Of course, the tool could not have landed on a flat clean surface. No, why would it when it could land on a pile of loose debris? Like a magnet picking up metal shavings, so the propolis-covered tool attracted dirt, twigs, leaves and grass. While picking up the tool, my propolis-covered glove attracted more debris. So much for being clean and neat. My frustration was building. I did not attempt to clean the tool or my glove. Why bother? If I tried to remove the debris from the tool or my dirty glove with my clean glove, then the clean glove would get dirty also. I needed to resume my inspection but could not do much about the sticky mess. If any debris fell into the open hive from my glove or the tool, then so be it. Of course, some debris did get into the hive. The housecleaning bees needed something to do. Besides it was a small price for them to pay for being entertained by my struggling with their glue.

Because of the headaches associated with propolis, beekeepers took action. When you want something, you go find it. If you cannot find it, then you make it. In the continual search for the perfect bee, beekeepers have been breeding bees for centuries. Bees with some desirable traits are bred with bees that have other good traits. Gentleness, disease resistance, low swarming tendency, effective pollination and good honey production are the main traits beekeepers desire in their bees. The perfect bee would have all of these traits and would also be one that collects and uses a minimal amount of propolis. There is a variation among races of bees regarding these traits as well as how much propolis they gather and use in their hives. Some beekeepers prefer certain races of bees over others simply based upon the limited amount of propolis used by the bees.

Regardless of the race of bee, there will always be some propolis present in the hive to annoy a beekeeper. But, despite the beekeeper's complaints, propolis does play a vital role for the bees as a means of securing the hive structure as well as creating a relatively disease-free environment. Within a church, problems will arise because people are present. The community members, even with all of their varied talents and gifts, can get on each other's nerves as personalities and styles conflict. But love is the glue that will hold everything together.

Love is an overused word in our society. People will say they "love" ice cream. Others might quip that they "love" their job. Fans will "love" their favorite sports team. Obviously these statements are meant to communicate a strong liking or attraction to a particular item. When people say they love their spouses or kids or parents, they are getting closer to the true meaning of love. When we look at love in the Bible, we need to start with God.

First John 4:8 tells us God is love. Love is but one of God's many attributes. Unfortunately many will focus solely on this attribute at the exclusion of God's other attributes, such as holiness (Isaiah 6:3) and justice (Job 5:1). A disproportionate emphasis on any of God's attributes will result in a distorted and incorrect view of who He is. But for now it is sufficient to know one of God's attributes is love.

God loves the entire world (John 3:16). Amazingly He loved us while we were His enemies (Romans 5:8-10). Once we accept His love and trust Christ alone for our salvation, nothing can ever separate us from God's love (Romans 8:38, 39). God's love is infinite (Psalm 103:11) as well as unconditional, embracing and accepting us despite our past and present unworthiness (Hosea 3:1). His love is the source of our love back to Him: we love Him because He first loved us (1 John 4:19).

Jesus told us that the top two commandments are, first, to love God with your whole being and, second, to love your neighbor as yourself (Matthew 22:37-40). Before discussing loving our neighbor (which in this context means to love fellow Christians), a little explanation is needed regarding what it means to love God with your whole being.

Deuteronomy 13:1-5 is where Moses warned the Israelites to be on guard against false prophets. Even if what the false prophets say comes to pass, the Israelites were not to listen to them. These false prophets were to be put to death because they were enticing the Israelites to follow false gods and thus rebel against God. There are two revealing verses in this section of Scripture—one stated negatively and the other stated positively. "*You shall not* listen to the words of that prophet or that dreamer of dreams; for the Lord your God is testing you to find out *if you love the Lord* your God with all your heart and with all your soul" (Deuteronomy 13:3). Evidently these false prophets served a purpose in God's plan—they tested the hearts of the Israelites. Would they follow God wholeheartedly, or would they go astray and seek after the enticements of the heathen gods and religions of the surrounding nations? Following anything or anyone but the true God is proof that one is not loving God.

The next verse provides the positive directive of loving God. "*You shall* follow the Lord your God and fear Him; and you shall keep His commandments, listen to His voice, serve Him, and cling to Him" (Deuteronomy 13:4). The key verbs are *follow, fear, keep, listen, serve* and *cling*. In the context of Deuteronomy the Israelites had the choice to *follow*

God or turn back to Egypt. God was on the move, and they could choose to go with Him or not. Today we need to identify what God is doing around us and get in tune with His program.[3] Like the Israelites we have a choice to make regarding whether we follow Him or not.

Fearing God is not being afraid of Him. Also it is more than a reverential respect. It involves an overwhelming and unspeakable sense of appreciating God for all that He is.[4] To try to explain this is impossible. Perhaps some imagery is the best that I can do: I would liken it to the sense of breathtaking admiration one might experience when beholding a stunning sunset, the crashing of the waves along the sea coast or the silent majesty of a snowcapped mountain. Such should be our response to our omniscient, omnipotent, sovereign God.

Keeping His commandments is self-evident. It only requires us knowing what they are. This is where a regular regiment of Bible reading is necessary. Do not worry about understanding it all the first time through. There are more than enough scriptural directives that we do understand to keep us busy for the rest of our lives. By continuously reflecting upon the Scriptures, however, we can learn as well as be reminded of what His commandments are.

If we are in tune with what God is doing, fearing Him, and are diligently keeping His Word, then we are in a good position to *listen* for His voice. This "voice" is when He gently addresses us in a personal way. I am not advocating that we need to hear an audible voice that provides specific direction for our life's journey. What I am advocating is that believers need to spend regular time in a place free of distractions to be still and seek God. During this seeking, God can gently impress upon us what He knows we need to "hear." Prayer is not talking *to* God. Prayer is talking *with* God. We need to make time in our prayer lives to listen to Him. Believers need to trust God's Spirit and allow Him the freedom to work in and through their hearts to communicate with them. God will never lead us in ways that are contrary to His nature or the Scriptures.

The sequence of the verbs in Deuteronomy 13:4 is significant. *Service* will follow listening. Let God lead you in a particular direction or to an area of service. But before you act or jump into service make sure you are in accordance with the Scriptures. Also being connected with other mature believers who know you well is very important. These godly friends should be able to provide objective and helpful feedback regarding what you believe God is leading you to do.

Finally, hold on! *Cling* to God. The New Testament parallel to clinging is abiding. In John 15 Jesus commands us to abide in Him like a branch abides in vine. If the branch becomes separated from the main trunk of the vine, it will wither and die. The connectedness between the branch and vine is meant to be unbroken. When Moses told the Israelites to cling to God it meant to not let go. Perhaps we should picture ourselves clinging to God as a frightened child would cling to the leg of a protective father.

Love first starts with God. He reached out to us. We respond by loving Him. Loving God means to put Him above all else. I challenge you to memorize and meditate upon Deuteronomy 13:4. Make it your theme verse in how you express your love for God as you live your life. Integrate Him into every part of your life and stay connected.

Because He unconditionally loves us, we can rest securely in His love. The more secure we are in God's love for us, the better we will be able to love others. "We love, because He first loved us. If someone says, 'I love God,' and hates his brother, he is a liar; for the one who does not love his brother whom he has seen, cannot love God whom he has not seen. And this commandment we have from Him, that the one who loves God should love his brother also" (1 John 4:19-21).

So how do we love one another? This book is based upon the parallels between the various functions bees perform within their colony and how a community of Christians should work together. In 1 Corinthians 12 Paul lists various spiritual gifts but tells us at the end of this chapter that there is still a better way. Paul then goes into what is called the "Love Chapter" of the Bible. Consider how *The Message* captures the importance of love and states what love is and what it is not:

> If I speak with human eloquence and angelic ecstasy but don't love, I'm nothing but the creaking of a rusty gate. If I speak God's Word with power, revealing all his mysteries

and making everything plain as day, and if I have faith that says to a mountain, "Jump," and it jumps, but I don't love, I'm nothing. If I give everything I own to the poor and even go to the stake to be burned as a martyr, but I don't love, I've gotten nowhere. So no matter what I say, what I believe, and what I do, I'm bankrupt without love.

Love never gives up. Love cares more for others than for self. Love doesn't want what it doesn't have. Love doesn't strut, doesn't have a swelled head, doesn't force itself on others, isn't always "me first," doesn't fly off the handle, doesn't keep score of the sins of others, doesn't revel when others grovel, takes pleasure in the flowering of truth, puts up with anything, trusts God always, always looks for the best, never looks back, but keeps going to the end. Love never dies.

It is difficult to find a more comprehensive and penetrating description of love than this. We could be highly skilled preachers and teachers, we could have earth-shaking faith, we could relinquish all of this world's good, and we could even make the ultimate sacrifice of laying down our lives as a martyr. It would all be meaningless without love. It is interesting to note that all of these admirable things just mentioned are highly individualistic in their nature. In other words, the focus is on "I." Love, however, must take place within community. The handling of propolis within the bee community is a team effort. When one bee brings this sticky substance into the hive, another bee must be present to help unload it.[5]

I hate to advocate the use of a checklist, but assess yourself against the criteria Paul put forth nearly two thousand years ago. Do not be surprised if you find yourself failing miserably. We all will. But do not lose heart. Remember that God's love for us is patient and unending and we can be thankful it is not dependent upon how well we love others. Let God's love for us be our motivation to love others. Love will cover a multitude of sins (1 Peter 4:8) and will be the glue that holds us together and will be a spiritual antiseptic counteracting the effects of pride and selfishness in our midst.

Someone said that, apart from what is necessary to sustain life, mankind's two greatest needs are *being loved* and *to love*. Love, despite its overuse as a word in our vocabulary, is the longing of every human heart and is therefore vitally important to the human experience. God knows this very well; after all, He made us in His image, and part of that image is love. The community of Christ's followers needs to reflect this image of God to the world. Perhaps this reflection of God is what Jesus had in mind when He said, "A new commandment I give to you, that you love one another, even as I have loved you, that you also love one another. By this all men will know that you are My disciples, if you have love for one another" (John 13:34-35). Love is the only sign provided by Jesus by which His disciples could be recognized.[6]

Propolis is a stubborn sticky substance that helps maintain a healthy environment and holds the beehive together. May we who are members of Christ's family stubbornly stick to one another in love so that nothing pulls us apart.

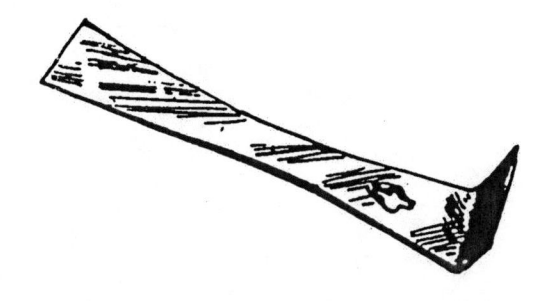

Figure 3: Hive tool (top) and frame gripper.
(Courtesy of Brushy Mountain Bee Farm Inc.)

Chapter 18

Influencing Your World

Perhaps one of the most visible yet unappreciated activities of the honeybee happens before our very eyes. We have all seen honeybees visiting flowers. It is what we do not see that is extremely important. While visiting flowers, the bees are participating in the act of pollination. Honeybees play an important role in the reproductive process in the plant kingdom and in doing so significantly help our food supply.

When gathering pollen the bees will collect the pollen from flowers and store it in pouches, called pollen baskets, located on their hind legs. In the early spring it is especially interesting to watch the bees returning to the hive with their full pollen baskets. Hungry for fresh food, the bees eagerly visit the various springtime flowers. The color of the pollen from these plants varies from almost white to a dark red depending upon the type of flower the bees visited. Typically when bees are out foraging they will tend to visit the same types of flowers or blossoms before moving on to another species. Because of this, bees are excellent agents of pollination among a given plant species.

As bees go from flower to flower, either searching for pollen or nectar, they will make contact with the pollen-bearing parts of the flower. Pollen is produced by the male parts of the plant which are called the anthers. Some of the pollen dust will fall off the anthers then stick to the fuzz of the bees' bodies. When the bees visit other flowers of the same variety, pollination will occur when some of the pollen dust falls from the bees and contacts the stigmas, the female parts of the flower. Thus, reproduction occurs within the plant kingdom.

Although they were interested in producing honey, pollination was taking place as ancient Egyptian beekeepers moved hives on rafts along the Nile River to follow fields that were coming into bloom. The first reference of honeybees being used for pollination, however, is found in the Koran (circa 600 A.D.) when hives were placed in date palm plantations.[1] Today in the United States large commercial beekeepers will winter their bees in the warmer Southern states. As the spring season progresses and warmer temperatures arrive, the locations of blossoming crops typically will move from region to region across the country. These commercial beekeepers will move their hives to follow these blossoming plants. Farmers will pay a fee to have beekeepers place hives near their crops for pollination. When the blossoms are past their peak, the beekeepers will pack up their hives and move on to pollinate the next type of blossoming plant. These

Bee Parables

beekeepers will move their bees up and down both coasts during the pollination season.

Occasionally a truck carrying these migrating beehives will be involved in an accident. The result is dozens of beehives strewn across the highway, millions of angry bees buzzing about and a highway closed down. Policemen and firemen may endure countless stings while assisting and removing the human victims from the accident scene. But the highway usually stays closed until the owners of the bees or local beekeepers arrive in full gear to clear the debris off the road and try to reassemble the scattered hive boxes. Every few years or so this scenario can be seen on an evening news broadcast.

Accidents aside, the beekeepers reap a twofold dividend. One is payment for their pollination services, and the other is the honey the bees produce while visiting these farms. The farmers' investment in pollination is rewarded in the form of larger crop yields. The first record of bees being rented for pollination in the United States was in 1909 for an apple orchard in New Jersey.[2] In simpler times before commercial beekeeping, farmers would keep bees themselves or be more than happy to allow other beekeepers to locate their hives on the farm year round. Honeybees have been known to fly as far as nine miles for food.[3] Since bees typically have a range of about two miles, a single hive can have a sphere of influence of over twelve square miles. Thus, a single hive of bees can pollinate a large area and help the crop yields of many farmers and gardeners.

Adequate pollination is a major concern of farmers. Without a good source of pollinators crop yields would be minimal, and the crops themselves may be smaller in size.[4] Pollination can result in an earlier crop. The sweetness and appearance of fruit is also affected by pollination. Today in the United States there are approximately 2.5 million colonies rented annually for pollination of crops that comprise about one-third of the American diet with these crops being are valued at over $14 billion.[5] Indeed these tiny creatures have a huge impact upon the human race because of their role in agriculture as pollinators. So between their roles in plant reproduction or in crop production bees have a tremendous influence on the world around them.

Christians are to be influencing the world around them. Influencing the world may seem to be an overwhelming task. But every one of us already has a sphere of influence which is admittedly a small part of the entire world. These many small spheres can collectively be quite large, though. Our spheres of influence are our households, extended family members, the neighborhood in which we live, our place of employment, social groups, political gatherings, hobby clubs, schools, sports teams, grocery stores, restaurants and vacation spots, to name a few. Anyone who crosses your path anytime in your life is a part of your sphere of influence.

Influencing people for Christ in its basic form is simply introducing others to Him. This can take place in many ways. It can occur in open air crusades, such as is done by Billy Graham, or as subtle as friendship evangelism that takes places over many years in many different settings. It can be as direct as inquiring about someone's spiritual heritage or as indirect as inviting someone over for dinner. One way to gauge your influence is to ask yourself, "When was the last time you had dinner with a nonbeliever?" or "How many friends do I have from outside the church?" Regardless of where we are or who we are with, we need to be sensitive to those around us, and most of all we need to be sensitive to the leading and prompting of God's Spirit within us. Pray for opportunities to introduce others to Christ and ask for wisdom on how to do it.

In keeping with the thought of bees and flowers, Paul uses the word *fragrance* in speaking of influencing the world. "But thanks be to God, who always leads us in triumph in Christ, and manifests through us the sweet aroma of the knowledge of Him in every place. For we are a *fragrance* of Christ to God among those who are being saved and among those who are perishing; to the one an aroma from death to death, to the other an aroma from life to life. And who is adequate for these things? For we are not like many, peddling the word of God, but as from sincerity, but as from God, we speak in Christ in the sight of God" (2 Corinthians 2:14-17).

When nonbelievers meet Christians, it is hoped the scent of Christ will be noticeable. To some it will be offensive. To others it will be the breath of life. How people respond to Christ is not our responsibility. Always remember it is their choice. You are called only to be a messenger. Evangelism is simply following Jesus' command to go (Mark 16:15) and claiming His promise of power (Acts 1:8). We just relay His message. Again, we are not responsible for how people respond. The only thing that believers must do is make themselves available.

Inevitably, when sharing Christ with others, objections will arise. If you can briefly address the objections, then by all means do so. If you do not know how to respond to a given question, then commit to finding an answer. This will show you are not a know-it-all and are honest and humble enough to admit your limits. Being genuine will go a long ways in influencing others. No one will ever have all of the answers to all of the objections people can raise. Try to be prepared as best you can.

When introducing others to Christ, try not to get sidetracked on peripheral issues such as church affiliation, scandalous headlines or even other religions. Keep Christ the focus of the discussion. Emphasize His life, death and especially His resurrection. Once while in a friendly two-and-a-half-hour spiritual discussion with a Buddhist on a plane flight I grew weary of our point/counterpoint exchange. Steve was quick of mind and had good questions and excellent comebacks. Finally I brought up Christ's resurrection. It stopped him cold in his tracks. Prior to this point he communicated that his world view was inclusive of all religions and we all would get to heaven because he believed we are all part of the same universal spiritual essence. Although he was an adherent to the ways of Buddha, he viewed the world's various religions as a smorgasbord—just pick whatever will work for you. When we got to the resurrection, I pointed out that from a strictly logical perspective the smorgasbord view seems deficient if one of the choices is not true. If Christ did not rise from the dead, then Christianity is based upon a hoax. Therefore, in selecting from among the world's religions, one must discard Christianity if it is not true. If Christ did rise from the dead, however, it then validates all of His claims, especially His claims to being God. At this point Steve paused for several seconds and said he did not know how to respond. Personally I was quite surprised at how powerful an impact the resurrection had on the conversation. As a Christian for over thirty years I was well aware of the resurrection of Christ as a fact in history. But never before this time had I realized how this one single point is so crucial to bring before others as they consider the religious landscape of our day.

In addition to historical evidence, do not neglect transformational evidence, that is, the evidence of changed lives and societies. Regarding the influence of Christianity in general throughout the world, some have observed the impact on entire regions of the world from various religions, most notably Northern Africa, the Middle East and Asia as compared to North America.[6] This may seem somewhat subjective or exaggerated. Although dated, consider these 1991 statistics as they pertain to the "10/40 Window" (this is the area across Africa and Asia from 10 to 40 degrees north latitude): ninety-seven percent of the least evangelized people live within this area; the major Muslim, Hindu and Buddhist countries are located here; eighty-two percent of the poorest of the poor reside here; and eighty-four percent of the people with the poorest quality of life are here.[7] Once while I was in a discussion with a devout atheist friend about the impact of Christianity upon the Western world, he readily acknowledged the stark contrast in the standard of living between regions of the world that have been influenced by Christianity and those regions that have not.

Perhaps these facts go unnoticed by most American Christians. We too easily have taken for granted the blessings we have, how we got them and the Source of their origin. We have more than enough of whatever we desire; yet we complain if we have to wait a few minutes in line at the grocery store. While a good portion of the world's population is simply trying to survive, we nervously watch the nightly business report from the comfort of plush furniture in our climate-controlled homes to see if our portfolios have inched higher or lower. If we do not feel well, we hop in our expensive cars and go to a well-educated doctor who prescribes a readily available medication or directs us to a highly trained specialist who will provide his services. Going without medical treatment or expecting a shortened life span due to rampant disease is par for the course in many places throughout the world. Have you ever given thought to the simple fact that you can read this sentence? Many in the world do not have an education and cannot read. Indeed we are truly the most blessed people the world has ever seen. Although the

Bee Parables

United States is in a post-Christian era, the influence Christianity has had on this country is undeniable.

For the sake of the world's people, especially those within our sphere of influence, let's commit to share the wonderful news of God's love and forgiveness that comes through Christ alone so they may experience the blessings of a transformed heart and life. Transformed individuals will transform communities and nations. I hope the following account will encourage you to spread the seeds of the gospel wherever you go regardless of how insignificant your efforts and influence may appear to be.

> I can never think of the boons and benefits the Bible invariably brings without thinking of Shimmabuke, a tiny village I came upon when, as a war correspondent, I was following on the heels of our troops beating out their tough and bloody victory on Okinawa.

> It was an obscure little community of only a few hundred native Okinawans. Thirty years before, an American missionary on his way to Japan had stopped here. He hadn't stayed long—just long enough to make a couple of converts, leave them a Bible and then pass on.

> One of the converts was Shosei Kina; the other was his brother Mojon. From the time of the missionary's visit, mind you, they had seen no other missionary, had no contact with any other Christian person or group. But in

those thirty years Shosei Kina and his brother Mojon had made that Bible come alive. Picking their way through its pages, they had found not only an inspiring Person on whom to pattern a life, but sound precepts on which to base their society.

Aflame with their discovery, they taught the other villagers until every man, woman and child in Shimmabuke was a Christian. Shosei Kina became head man in the village; his brother Mojon, the chief teacher. In Mojon's school, the Bible was read daily. To Shosei Kina's village government, its precepts were law. This Book was their literature, their moral code, their final court of appeal for all the problems of living. And under the impact of this Book pagan things had fallen away. In their place, during these thirty years, there had developed a Christian democracy at its purest—a democracy that the Japanese occupation forces, moving in to fortify the island, could neither understand nor shake.

Then after thirty years came the American Army, storming across the island. Little Shimmabuke was directly in their path and took some severe shelling. When our advance patrols swept up to the village compound, the GIs, their guns leveled, stopped dead in their tracks as two little old men stepped forth, bowed low and began to speak.

An interpreter explained that the old men were welcoming them as fellow Christians. They had heard the Americans were on their way; they remembered that their missionary had come from America. So, though these Americans seemed to approach things a little differently than had the missionary, the two old men were overjoyed to see them.

The GIs' reaction was typical. Flabbergasted, they sent for their chaplain.

The chaplain came, and with him officers of the intelligence service. They toured the village and were astounded at what they saw—the spotlessly clean homes and streets, the poise and gentility of the villagers, the high level of health and happiness, intelligence and prosperity of Shimmabuke. They had seen many other villages on Okinawa—villages of unbelievable poverty and ignorance and filth. Against these, Shimmabuke shone like a diamond on a dungheap.

Shosei Kina and his brother Mojon observed the Americans' amazement and took it for disappointment. They bowed humbly and said: "We are sorry if we seem a backward people. We have, honored sirs, tried our best to follow the Bible and live like Jesus. Perhaps if you will show us how...."

Show them?

I strolled through Shimmabuke one day with a tough old Army sergeant. As we walked he turned to me and whispered hoarsely, "I can't figure it, fellow—this kind of people coming out of only a Bible and a couple of old guys who want to live like Jesus!" Then he added what was to me an infinitely penetrating observation: "Maybe we've been using the wrong kind of weapons to make the world over!"[8]

Chapter 19

Multiplication by Division

The way the honeybee species multiplies is when individual colonies divide in two. Although a queen bee may lay over one thousand eggs per day to maintain a strong colony, the species' survival depends upon the number of colonies that exist. When a colony splits, it is called swarming. When a swarm occurs, the queen and a large portion of the colony leave the comfort and familiarity of their hive to venture out and start a new home. Those bees that remain behind continue to use the hive as their base of operation.

A swarm occurs when the existing queen, along with about two-thirds of the colony members,[1] leaves the hive to find another place to live. The swarming process is complicated and begins a few weeks before the queen and her followers actually leave their well-established home. First, it is believed that swarming is prompted by excessive congestion in the brood area. When this occurs, the workers will select ten to twenty freshly laid eggs and prepare them to develop into queen bees. When the eggs hatch, the workers will feed the young larvae a special food called royal jelly that will cause them to develop into queens. The cells in which these special larvae are developing are made much larger than normal worker cells and even that of drone cells. In its final form the capped queen cell has an external texture similar to that of the outside of a peanut shell.

From the time these selected eggs are laid to the time when a queen bee emerges is sixteen days. (Worker bees emerge after twenty-one days, and drones emerge after twenty-four days.) Four or five days before the new queens emerge from their cells, however, several things happen. The existing queen bee will go on a diet of sorts and stop laying eggs so she will lose about one-third of her body weight and thus be able to fly with the swarm.[2] Meanwhile, the bees that will leave the hive start tanking up on honey for the upcoming journey. No one exactly knows how the colony determines which bees swarm with the queen or which ones remain at the hive. However, after the queen is able to fly, she and her brave volunteers leave the hive about a day or two before the new queens begin to emerge.

When the swarm initially leaves the hive, the bees will gather on a low-hanging branch about fifty to one hundred feet from the hive. There they will cluster in a mass that can be about the size of a volleyball. They may stay there for a few hours or maybe even a day. In the meantime, scout bees are out and about searching for a new home. When they find a potential home, the scouts return to the cluster and pass on the information to the others by doing a dance on the surface of the cluster. The dance communicates distance and direction. Only the bees in the immediate vicinity of the dance will get this information. The amazing thing about this process is that there are believed to be multiple scouts finding multiple potential homes. Therefore, when each scout returns it will do a different dance from the other scouts because they found different prospective homes at different locations. Also, the scouts will be reporting their information to different groups of bees in the cluster. Despite the various reports from multiple scouts, no one knows how the swarm of bees ultimately decides where to go nor is it understood how they will all end up at the same location.

Once situated in their new home the bees get to work. They clean their home by hauling out any loose debris and sealing unwanted holes or cracks. The bees will begin making wax to build the comb that will cradle future generations of workers. The comb that is made will also be used to store food for survival through the coming winters. Within a few days the queen will begin laying eggs as the comb building progresses. A swarm is comprised mostly of younger bees which are between four to twenty-three days old.[3] This youth movement is probably because younger bees are the primary producers of wax, for comb building, and royal jelly, for feeding the new larvae. Meanwhile older bees are foraging about to gather pollen and nectar for food since the food they brought from the old hive has now been exhausted. Now, with things well underway, the life cycle of this new colony can begin.

Meanwhile back at the old hive, the new queens are beginning to emerge from their cells. Since there can only be one queen in the hive, conflict will occur. The queen bee that emerges first will find the other queens that are still in their cells, and she will plunge her stinger through the cell walls and kill the queen bees within. The queen bee's stinger is different from a worker bee's stinger. The worker bee's stinger is barbed and remains hooked in its target. When the worker bee pulls away from the target, the stinger, along with the bee's intestines, remains attached to the target. Without its intestines the worker bee will die. The queen's stinger, however, is basically straight and can be withdrawn from its target without harm being done to her when she stings. If two queens emerge at the same time, they will fight to the death. The winner of the fight will then be the next queen of the hive. The new queen will then have to mate in order to be able lay fertilized eggs to begin to replace the hive's work force that was lost due to the swarm.

It should be noted that both the home colony and the new colony will probably not produce any excess honey due to the disruption caused by swarming.[4] Also sometimes a colony will malfunction, as it were, by generating multiple successive swarms for no apparent reason. Because the hive population drops due to swarming, each subsequent swarm becomes smaller and weaker all the while depleting the home colony of bees. In cases like this, the chances for survival diminish both for the swarms as well as for the home hive.[5]

European bee colonies may generate a few swarms each year. Sometimes they do not generate any. Typically the average is one per year. Swarming generally occurs before July. It is believed that after the spring equinox, when the days start to become shorter, the bees may know it is too late in the season for a swarm to be successful.[6] If they start any later in the season, there may not be adequate time or opportunity to prepare for the coming winter. Africanized bees ("killer" bees), which thrive in hot climates, are more prolific than their European counterparts and therefore swarm more frequently. Thus, one can understand the progressive and eventual spreading of this species of bees from Brazil up to the southern United States. More will be discussed about killer bees later. Swarming is the method, however, by which honeybees propagate their species. If swarming did not occur, the number of colonies would eventually decline until the existing colonies perished from disease or disaster. Swarming is a normal and natural event in the life of a colony.

Regarding the propagation of the Christian faith, Jesus provided the Great Commission. He said, "All authority has been given to Me in heaven and on earth. Go therefore and make disciples of all the nations, baptizing them in the name of the Father and the Son and the Holy Spirit, teaching them to observe all that I commanded you; and, lo, I am with you always, even to the end of the age" (Matthew 28:18-20).

It is an amazing thing to realize a movement that started with twelve men has spread to every continent and claims billions of followers. The key to their success was to "make disciples." What is a disciple? In the New Testament period disciples were those who served their teachers hoping one day to become master teachers themselves.[7] Thus, being a disciple of Christ means to serve Him and to become like Him (Romans 8:29). Making disciples is not the same as adding members to the church rolls or getting a church's attendance to increase. Making disciples is hard work. It is a long-term investment in people with the hope of future multiplication being the ultimate result as the disciples implement the ministry skills they learned from their teachers.

Despite the growth of Christianity from its humble beginnings, today there are many who have never heard of Jesus. Those who have never heard are not just those in some remote corner of the globe but include our neighbors, coworkers and classmates here in America. Believe it or not, there is an ever increasing number of Americans who have no understanding of who Jesus is or what He did. America, which once had a rich Christian heritage, is for the most part in a post-Christian era. The Christian church, which once held an esteemed position in our culture, is now being pushed to the fringes by those who shout "separation of church and state" and by those who accuse Christians of intolerance.

How did the decline of the church's influence and prestige occur? One can point to many factors. There was the introduction of liberalism into American churches and seminaries at the beginning of the twentieth century which led to the degradation of the authority of Scripture. In recent times, postmodernism has certainly been an obstacle for the church because it challenges all authority, dismisses absolutes and embraces everything (except absolutes). Of course, church leaders involved with sex scandals and child molestations have significantly undermined the cause of Christ. But the church itself may be its own biggest problem. It seems that in any area of life, if one is not advancing, expanding or taking the offensive, then one is therefore resigned to retreating, shrinking or being on the defensive. How many times have we watched our favorite sports team gain a big lead early in the game by playing aggressively and then watch that lead deteriorate as they begin to play conservatively while their opponent stages a comeback?

Comfort and convenience have taken the edge off the church's commitment to fulfill the Great Commission. Although this was not necessarily a deliberate effort, it nonetheless is how things turned out. Numerical growth in membership is usually a good problem to have. From a human standpoint there is safety in numbers and, hence, some of the appeal of a larger church. But Jesus did not tell us to be safe. He told us to go.

But instead of training and instilling a mindset of spiritual multiplication within the masses, churches have tried to accommodate the increasing membership with multiple services or bigger church buildings. Large churches are not a bad thing as they can do many things smaller churches cannot. When a particular church grows numerically, however, more often than not it is simply "sheep stealing" or "reshuffling the deck" of the local Christian population within a given area.

In the corporate world motivational speakers are brought in basically to brainwash the employees with the message the corporate leadership wants to send. A common theme of these speakers nowadays pertains to change. "Change is your friend." "Embrace change." "With change comes opportunity." Blah, blah, blah. The underlying reason for the need to put on this dog-and-pony show is simple—people do not like to change. We all get stuck in our ways to various degrees and dig in our heels when someone or something suggests or forces us to change. The same is true with any church. There are reasons why people attend the churches they do. They like the pastor or priest. They like his teaching. They like the worship style or music. They like the friends they have made at the church. The list could go on, but the bottom line is that people like what they like and do not want it to change.

Consider the church at Antioch in the book of Acts. Could you imagine attending a church that simultaneously had Paul, Barnabas and Silas as leaders? From a teaching perspective it could not get any better. But instead of staying in Antioch in a holy huddle, these men left Antioch to preach the gospel and plant churches. From Acts we know Paul did not play it safe but instead experienced many hardships as he spread the gospel. He was beaten, stoned, imprisoned, maligned, rejected, abandoned and ultimately executed. Retirement to a comfortable beachfront bungalow somewhere on the sunny and warm Mediterranean seashore was not an option for Paul.

Speaking of Paul, let's consider his advice for a model of ministry. "The things which you have heard from me in the presence of many witnesses, entrust these to faithful men who will be able to teach others also" (2 Timothy 2:2). Paul's advice was simple: The teachings of the faith were to be passed on to faithful, qualified and committed people (disciples) who in turn would pass them on to others. Where do you usually find this caliber of people? They are the meat-and-potato folks who comprise the bulk of church membership today. These people did not become spiritually mature overnight. They are the product of a pipeline of Christian education and mentoring that included hundreds of sermons, numerous conferences and retreats, time spent studying the Scriptures, hours of prayer and devotions, and countless interactions with other believers that involved sharing life's struggles and victories.

There is a vast reservoir of Christians that can be, and should be, utilized to help fulfill the Great Commission. Instead of seeing oneself first as an engineer, teacher, student, mechanic or stay-at-home-mom, everyone should see themselves as a missionary cleverly disguised as an engineer, teacher, student, mechanic or stay-at-home-mom. Each believer has his or her own unique sphere of influence (mission field) that God has given them. With the support and encouragement of other believers, Christians should be reaching out to impact their part of the world.

One of the major reasons that cause a colony to swarm is overcrowding. A strong healthy honeybee colony will begin to make the necessary preparations to swarm. At the proper time the split occurs. The old queen and her followers set out to establish a new hive. The remaining members of the original hive will rally behind the new queen to replenish the workers that left. Both of these two colonies are weaker than when they were one and thus run the risk of not being adequately prepared for the coming winter as a result of the smaller work force. Nevertheless, both colonies' members will strive to do their individual jobs to help ensure the survival of their respective colonies.

This should be what goes on within a church. When a church is healthy it will grow, and overcrowding will result. Instead of knocking down walls or breaking ground to build a bigger sanctuary, it should consider planting another church. An expanding church should reach a point where an organized split can occur to create additional ministry partners—not competitors. Within a healthy growing church there should be the stirring of God's Spirit among its members. This stirring will take place over time, and then at the right instance a new ministry can be birthed, resulting in two ministry partners where there was once only one. Granted, both will be numerically and financially weaker than when they were united. But this weakened condition may create exactly what many churches and Christians do not always practice—a complete trust and dependence upon God.

Having a few large colonies of bees is not in the best interests of the honeybee species. The more colonies that exist will increase the likelihood for survival of the species. Likewise, a few huge churches may not be in the best long-term interests of expanding God's kingdom in a given area. Both small and large churches have their pros and cons. Regardless of the size, healthy churches will always be mindful of Christ's words to go into all the world and make disciples.

Chapter 20

Cutting Edge

One of the roles bees perform is scouting. Typically bees have a range of about two miles. In some cases they have been known to fly up to nine miles! Numerous scout bees fly about searching for supplies for the hive. These bees will search for nectar, pollen, propolis and water. When the scout bees are successful and find what they are looking for, they return to the hive and perform a dance which communicates direction and distance to the others. The liveliness of the dance and the quality of any samples determine whether the scouts will be successful in gaining any recruits to heed their advice. Scout bees are also used to find a new home for a swarm that has just left the comfort and familiarity of their hive. Regardless of whether they are searching for supplies or a new home, scout bees play an important role within their community. They search the countryside looking for things to fulfill the need of the colony and then return home to provide a report. This information is vital to the success of the colony.

Experiments performed by the late Noble Prize winner Professor Karl von Frisch indicated that bees can be trained. He conducted experiments which indicated that bees can distinguish colors and scents. For example, von Frisch would place a feeding station on a table of a given color. Scout bees from a hive would find the feeding station and return to the hive to inform others. Quickly the bees associated the food with the color of the table. He then would place other feeding stations on tables of different colors near the original table and feeding station. The bees readily ignored the other tables and would return to the original feeding station. Professor von Frisch conducted similar experiments with comparable results that trained the bees to distinguish scents. When bees were evaluated regarding both color and scent, it was determined that from a distance color was important but ultimately the bees went to a feeding station based upon scent. The fact that bees can make these distinctions does make sense when one realizes that in the search for food bees will seek certain flowers over others based upon color and scent.[1]

Knowing honeybees can be trained, the Department of Defense has sought a military application. I first became aware of this while watching one of the educational cable channels. At one of the national laboratories bees were being trained to find land mines. The show did not go into a lot of detail about how they were doing this. It looked somewhat humorous, though, seeing explosives piled next to a feeding station covered with bees. The experimenters were training the bees to associate food with the scent of explosives. The explosives emit a faint odor that cannot be detected by humans but is discernable by the bees.

Once the bees graduated from boot camp, their hive was taken to a test site where land mines or explosives were in the vicinity. The bees were released from the hive and then would go out scouting for the scent of explosives. As bees forage, they attract particles of dust, soil and pollen to their fuzzy statically charged bodies and bring samples back to the hive. Researcher Jerry Bromenshenk, of the University of Montana at Missoula, said that "bees are like flying dust mops."[2] If a bee found explosives, trace amounts of the scent would adhere to its body. Upon returning to the hive, a bee would pass through a sensitive explosive detector that would inform the experimenters the bee had found the explosives.

Knowing if an area was clear of land mines or other explosives would be useful information to the military. They would know whether or not it was safe to move troops or vehicles into or through a given area. But, equally important, officials would know if it was safe for civilians to move back into an area after the combatants had departed. The late Princess Diana vigorously campaigned against land mines because of the needless death and injury they cause to innocent civilians. Based upon 1999 data, approximately sixty people were maimed or killed daily by land mines. Also the Red Cross estimated that 80-120 million land mines were deployed in seventy countries with about 40,000 additional land mines deployed each week.[3]

I did not recall that the show explained how the experimenters would be able to locate these explosives, but at least the bees were able to help them determine the presence of explosives. Some internet articles mentioned attaching small diodes onto the backs of trained bees while using handheld radar tracking devices to follow the bees[4] or developing a laser tracking system to map where the bees go.[5] A fiscal 2007 defense appropriations bill included five million dollars for continued research in using bees to find explosives. Besides explosives, the sky is the limit as bees could be trained to find almost anything.[6]

Who would have thought scout bees would be drafted into the armed services!?

As you can see, scouting is a means of gathering information to help in the decision-making process. In the Old Testament there are several examples of scouting. In Genesis Noah sent birds, a raven and a dove (8:6-12), to look for dry land. In Numbers Moses sent twelve men to scout out the Promised Land (13:1-20). Nehemiah went out at night on a reconnaissance mission to assess the condition of the Jerusalem wall (2:12-16). In the New Testament Paul sent Timothy as a scout to ascertain the condition of various churches (Philippians 2:19; 1 Thessalonians 3:6). In keeping with the biblical example, as well as learning from the bees, the church today needs to use scouts to seek out and gather information to help make informed ministry decisions.

Scouts in the church today are not just those who are on a church building committee looking for a prime piece of real estate to locate a new sanctuary. There are those who scan news reports to try to tie biblical prophecies to current events with the intent of warning people the end is near. Concerned Christians cautioned us about what might have happened on midnight of January 1, 2000, if the Y2K bug struck. Although these are examples of Christian scouting efforts, the most important scouts are those whose efforts have application in the day-to-day activities of believers and the church.

These largely unheralded scouts are those forward-looking individuals who assess what is going on in the world and seek to incorporate it into the ministry of the church. Such scouts include those that minister on college campuses. They choose to minister in such places because the next generation of influential government and corporate leaders are found there. Other scouts keep abreast of current cultural phenomenon such as *The DaVinci Code* because they wanted believers to be able to respond intelligently to the questions and confusion generated by this high-profile murder mystery. These individuals also tried to encourage the church to use this issue as an opportunity to communicate the gospel. Still other scouts will monitor the culture for broad but significant trends, such as postmodernism, and attempt to get the church up to speed on what it is, how it affects peoples' thinking and what Christians should do to deal with it.

Granted not every Christian shares in the enthusiasm and passion these scouts have for their field of interest. But Christians should be aware of significant trends or events occurring in the world around them. One worth exploring in a little detail is that of postmodernism. Postmodernism will affect the way ministry will be conducted in this country for the foreseeable future. Therefore it is imperative that believers are aware of this phenomenon and try to understand it.

Postmodernism is difficult to define. Perhaps it is better described than defined. Generally speaking, postmodernism is a world view that is foreign to most modernists. (Those of us who are older tend to lean more toward modernism than postmodernism.) Postmodernists value diversity and authenticity. They embrace relativism—there is no one right way. They are largely anti-authority. They are highly individualistic in their thinking. Combining these attributes, postmodernists will say something to the effect of "What works for you might not work for me. That's okay because what works for me might not work for you." As you can tell, postmodernists are not big on passing judgment on others, nor do they take kindly to those who pass judgment on them or anyone else. They are intrigued by mystery. They do not like to be told about truth. Instead they want to figure it out for themselves and are thus fond of stories or movies or even parables as a means of learning. Postmodernists may not necessarily follow a set method whereas modernists tend to seek standardization and are more process-oriented. For the postmodernist, A + B + C will not always equal D. Despite their individualistic and somewhat unstructured and unpredictable approach to life, postmodernists place a high value on relationships and being part of a group or community.[7]

If the church wants to be effective and relevant in society, it must try to understand the nuances and ramifications of this world view. Perhaps we all need to be like "the sons of Issachar, men who understood the times, with knowledge of what Israel should do" (1 Chronicles 12:32). These men had the insight to see that David would be king over Israel and chose to align themselves accordingly. Believers today need to recognize what is going on around them and respond appropriately.

Two major paradigm shifts have to occur within the traditional church to better deal with postmodernism. First, the day of mass evangelism is closing rapidly. Big revivals, gatherings, crusades, tent meetings and gospel tracts will probably have limited effectiveness. Even relying upon a professional Christian such as a pastor, priest or staff person from a parachurch group to spread the gospel will have limited results. These types of outreach events and Christian workers are generally not embraced in postmodern thinking. Although the message put out by these traditional means was, is and will always be valid, the method of delivery may need to change based upon the audience.

The key to influencing postmodernists will rest with individual Christians. "Average" Joe and Josephine Christian need to be ready, willing and able to spend a lot of one-on-one time with postmodernists. There will need to be a genuine effort by Christians to develop meaningful friendships with those outside the faith. Believers need to shed the "pop-it-in-the-microwave" mentality and think in terms of long-term investing. Sharing a gospel tract is on the way out. Genuinely living the message of the gospel has to occur. Thus, in order for the message of the gospel to go forth today, individual Christians must step up to the challenge of doing ministry within their sphere of influence. Ministry responsibilities, such as evangelism and discipleship, that were once largely shouldered by professional Christian workers must now be carried by the laity.

The second paradigm shift that needs to be understood is that of the involvement of postmodernists with a local church. In the past, people generally first came to faith in Christ, and then they became part of a church family. In other words one believed before belonging. With postmodernists, the opposite will probably occur—they will want to belong before they believe. Because postmodernists value community with others they may attend a local church on their own volition as they seek to be part of a group. The good news is they came to church. The bad news is the church may not know how to deal with them. These new attendees will want to have an active role in the church by volunteering to serve within the church and by being on various committees. Postmodernists coming into the church will bring with them all of their philosophies and values, some of which may run contrary to biblical Christianity. Believers within the church will have to walk the fine line of accepting these people while not accepting all of their views. Christians must bear in mind that they too did not have their theology all worked out when they first came to faith in Christ. Therefore they need to be patient with those who attend their church but are not yet believers. Christian leaders will be challenged in their art of diplomacy as they stand committed to Christ while communicating with those of a different world view. It is hoped Christians will apply wisdom and grace in these potentially contentious situations.

Some Christians and churches are already aware of and dealing with postmodernism. Many are not. Jesus told His followers to "go into all the world" (Mark 16:15). This command is still relevant to His followers today. The act of leaving the comfort and familiarity of one's Christian environment and friends to venture out into the world of those outside the church can be uncomfortable. A few years ago my wife and I realized the only people we socialized with were Christians from our church. This was not bad in and of itself. But we realized we were leading a selfish and somewhat sheltered life. Jesus did not give us the message of eternal life to hide it under a basket (Matthew 5:15) by hanging out only with other believers. As His followers we needed to honor Him by taking His message to those around us. In a matter of a few months our social life had completely changed. We were spending time almost exclusively with those outside the church. We still attended church, maintained contact with other believers and supported various missionary organizations. But we felt it was necessary to spend time with those in our sphere of influence and plant the seeds of the gospel. By doing this we have found our interactions with those folks from outside our church to be interesting and personally enriching experiences.

Some honeybee scouts find better sources of supplies than others. It is to the benefit of the entire colony that the members pursue the best sources available. Ultimately the success of the whole colony depends heavily upon how the members respond to the information provided by the scout bees. So too must the church give audience to its scouts and respond in the most effective and appropriate manner to further God's kingdom.

Chapter 21

Killer Bees

The term "killer bees" was coined in the mid-1960s. It was applied to bees that descended from African honeybee queens accidentally released from a breeding experiment being conducted in Brazil in 1956. In Brazil they were called the "assassin" bee which was translated outside the country as the "killer" bee.[1] Breeding various species of bees is not a new concept. Beekeepers breed different varieties of honeybees in an effort to develop new ones that will have the most desirable characteristics. The purpose of this experiment in Brazil was to develop a honeybee that could live in the hot and humid Amazon region because European bees were not able to do so. The experiment's ultimate goal was to establish a beekeeping industry in that area.

Professor Warwick E. Kerr was the individual responsible for this experiment. Kerr got a bad wrap from the government because of the unplanned escape of these queen bees. In 1964 the military took over the Brazilian government. Kerr was an outspoken opponent of the new regime. Because Kerr was internationally known for his work in the beekeeping industry, the new government was reluctant to come down too hard on him. Instead, since they controlled the media, Kerr was the object of a smear campaign to discredit him. It is true African bees are more easily provoked than European bees, and therefore they are more likely to sting people or animals. But the government exaggerated stories of any stinging incident (whether caused by honeybees or other stinging insects) and associated them with Kerr. Thus, the legend of the "killer bees" is more fiction than fact. There have been no such stories coming out of Africa.[2]

African bees may swarm more often than European bees. (A typical European bee colony usually swarms once a year.) However, an African bee swarm may fly over one hundred miles. Thus, it was only a matter of time before these African bees spread and made their way to the United States. On October 15, 1990, a swarm of these bees was found in southern Texas. As the African bees moved north, it is believed they bred to some extent with European bees along the way and their temperament may have mellowed somewhat. *Africanized* bees are bees with some Africa descent as opposed to *African* bees which are solely African in descent. Without going into a lot of detail, these Africanized bees are more aggressive in tropical climates and behave more like European bees in temperate climates. In appearance the African and European bees are almost identical except that the African bees are about ten percent smaller. Their venom glands are smaller also, but there is no difference in the venom.

Bee Parables

Beekeepers that work with Africanized bees take special precautions. First, they will locate their hives away from towns or villages. They will use good protective clothing. Futhermore, they will use bigger smokers to ensure an ample supply of smoke to calm the bees. Beekeepers will be more mindful of conditions that are irritating to the bees and thus avoid handling them during those times. Those times include extended rainy periods or times of low food supply when the bees are hungry. Also extremely hot days are not good times to get into a hive. But overall working with Africanized bees is no different from working with European bees except for the extra precautions.

Even though there may not be a significant impact upon beekeepers, Africanized bees can still be a threat to people in general. There are about one hundred thousand stinging incidents annually in the United States. About fifty people die annually from these stinging incidents. (By comparison, about eight thousand individuals are bitten by venomous snakes resulting in about twelve deaths annually in the United States.[3]) With the continuing northward spread of African bees, fatalities are expected to double in the future. Fatalities from stings usually occur due to a strong allergic reaction. But numerous stings can result in a toxic reaction. The seriousness of the response depends upon a person's overall health. One individual was stung over twenty-two hundred times and survived.[4]

Although, Professor Kerr's experiment did not go exactly as he had planned, there is now a well-established African honey bee presence in the steamy Amazon River Basin to support a beekeeping industry. Overall, the Africanized bees are efficient pollinators and honey producers. They are very hard workers but are somewhat uptight.

Who are the "killer bees" of the Christian community?

This section of the book is probably going to offend some folks as their deep rooted views and values will be challenged. But read the entire chapter carefully before making a final assessment. The "killer bees" are legalistic Christians. These believers can unintentionally harm themselves and others. The author is a recovering legalist.

What is a legalist? There may be technical or theological definitions floating about. But I will define a legalist as the way I had lived my life. A legalist is anyone who tries to measure one's standing before God by what he or she does. It is trying to gauge an internal spiritual condition by applying external standards. A little explanation at this point is necessary.

According to biblical Christianity, one becomes a Christian by placing his or her trust in Christ as Savior and Lord. It is only through trusting His death and resurrection that we have forgiveness of our sins and are declared righteous or blameless in the eyes of God. Most professing Christians will agree with this and acknowledge that salvation cannot be earned by anything we do. It is a gift from God that we must individually receive by faith through our own individual conscious decision. This gift is free to all who trust Him (Ephesians 2:8-9). It is truly the most wonderful news the world has ever heard. God's grace is truly amazing.

As time goes on, new Christians will become integrated into a community of believers. They will receive teaching and see the example of other Christians. Unless one is careful, the simple trust and devotion that inaugurated their Christian journey will begin to fade and will be replaced with the labor of self-effort. Legalistic Christians start out with good intentions but become lost in the forest of Christian activities. Good works are indeed a trademark of a genuine Christian as Jesus Himself said "you will know them by their fruits" (Matthew 7:20). But what seems to happen is that a life of trust and devotion to Christ is replaced with a mental checklist of expected actions or behaviors. This checklist is not something most churches hand out to their members. This checklist is internal (and unique) to each person and becomes a guide by which they live their lives. There are usually many good things on these checklists: reading the Bible, prayer, church attendance, Scripture memory, fasting, helping the poor, financially contributing to various ministries and going on missionary trips, to name a few.

No doubt these ideals and disciplines have been passed down through generations of Christians. There is nothing wrong with these activities in and of themselves. In fact, these are excellent disciplines of the Christian life. The issue, though, is the reliance upon the fulfillment of the checklist that is the root of several problems. First, these lists should not replace the role of the Holy Spirit as our guide (Galatians

3:3). Second, the completion (or lack thereof) of this checklist should not become an indicator of our position in Christ. Third, one can grow very weary trying to do everything on the list. Finally, people's lists seem to grow to include a lot of things that certainly are not absolutes of the faith. For example, people and churches will take stands on issues such as drinking alcohol, smoking or dancing. Certain movies are out of bounds. Companies are boycotted because of their position on certain moral or social issues. Some only invest in "morally responsible" stocks or mutual funds. The list could go on and on and on and on. The point is that one could spend his or her entire life analyzing everything and taking all sorts of stands or positions on issues. Yes, we do need to be careful how we live our lives. Paul encourages us to live by our convictions (Romans 14:22). But when we place such high emphasis on our personal convictions that they become absolutes of our faith by which we judge ourselves and others, then we have crossed way over the line of grace and are firmly into legalism.

As a point to ponder, consider what someone said about the *convictions* (not *absolutes*) we hold: "Our convictions are a reflection of our view of God." Do we view God as a cosmic killjoy or as a loving Father? Do we see God as stifling and monotonous or as expressive and creative? In my personal journey I was viewing God more as a strict taskmaster than a loving father. This view of God was building a barrier between Him and me while the convictions I held were likewise building barriers instead of bridges with people—Christians and non-Christians alike.

How do you view God? Brennan Manning writes: "The God of the legalistic Christian ... is often unpredictable, erratic and capable of all manner of prejudices. When we view God this way, we feel compelled to engage in some sort of magic to appease Him. Sunday worship becomes a superstitious insurance policy against His whims. This God expects people to be perfect and to be in perpetual control of their feelings and thoughts. When broken people with this concept of God fail—as inevitably they must—they usually expect punishment. So they persevere in religious practice as they struggle to maintain a hollow image of a perfect self. The struggle is exhausting. The legalist can never live up to the expectations they project on God."[5]

Your view of God will determine how you live your life. Maybe you do not go overboard with your checklist, but nonetheless you may be leaning to some extent upon your list as an indicator of your standing with God. Consider the following "Christian résumé—attended church throughout the week, memorized Scripture, regularly shared your faith, discipled/trained others to become disciplers, participated in countless church committees, taught in a Bible college, spoke at Christian seminars across the country, did a daily fifteen-minute Christian radio broadcast, founder and president of a ministry, authored numerous Bible study booklets, director of evangelism at one of the country's largest churches, headed a citywide evangelistic outreach.

Impressed? Despite this amazing résumé, Bob George, while stuck in a traffic jam one day, broke down and wept because he was absolutely miserable.[6] In his book *Classic Christianity* he explained what went wrong and how he got back on track. In fact, he went on to continue living his résumé but with renewed vigor because this time he was not alone. What was his problem? In a nutshell he was too busy with the things of God and had drifted far from his first love. His solution was a rediscovery of God's love and grace.

From this example it is easy to see that one can do the right things but for the wrong reasons. Evangelists will claim Christianity is not just a religion—a set of creeds and rituals—but a relationship with an all-knowing, all-powerful, loving God. After becoming a Christian, believers seem, to varying degrees, to lean more toward the activities or disciplines of the faith rather than to the Author of the faith. The disciplines of the Christian faith were never meant to interfere with our relationship with God.[7] Manning notes, "The American church today accepts grace in theory but denies it in practice.... The emphasis shifts from what God is doing to what we are doing."[8] Initially there may be a "high" of accomplishing some of these Christian disciplines. But after a while the excitement fades, and drudgery sets in. Some try to gut it out. They will persevere for years by laying claim to the promises that await them after death—all the while they are dying on the inside and too afraid to admit it. Others silently come to the conclusion that it is just not worth it. Their rationale is simple: "If this is the abundant life, then you can have it." These people then quietly fade into the background and follow Christ only from a distance, if at all. Those outside the Christian community see this occurring and can discern these are not happy people. Legalism harms and hides the true message of the Good News.

Where does legalism come from? To a large extent, legalism stems from our inherent sinful nature that wants to be independent of God. It seems paradoxical that sin could be prompting us to do godly things but in actuality we may be doing the right thing for the wrong reason.

Living in a performance-based society like America can certainly plant the seeds of legalism. It starts in our early childhood when our parents punish bad behavior and praise good behavior. In school, grades are based upon performance. Starting positions on a sports team or leading roles in a play are earned based upon performance. Entrance into college is based upon high school grades and national test scores. Getting an interview with a potential employer is largely based upon one's class standing or past experience. If hired, a new employee will have to go through a probation period in which continued employment is contingent upon adequate performance. Raises and bonuses are linked to performance. In other words, if one does not perform well in our secular society, then privileges and benefits could be lost. It is only a very small mental step to apply this mindset to the Christian faith. In fact, notice how performance is highlighted in ministry newsletters or updates as they seek to maintain or gain donor support.

Perhaps another thing that can lead to a performance-based faith is the concept of rewards. The Bible clearly teaches that each of us will receive a reward from the Lord according to what we have done (1 Corinthians 3:8). Thus, there is a component of performance on our part that correlates to how God will respond to us. But this should not be confused with the fact that we are still His precious adopted children (Romans 8:15), and that can never change.

How do we get back on track? We go back to the basics. As I reflect upon my high school football days, the reason for our losses was due to our poor performance in the basics—blocking, tackling, hanging on to the ball. Forget the double reverse or the halfback option pass. We were our own worst enemy. We were not beaten by our opponents. We beat ourselves because we failed to execute the basics. Paul admonished his readers about going back to important fundamentals. Philippians 3:1 says, "To write the same things again is no trouble to me, and it is a safeguard for you." How do Christians "beat themselves"? They forget the greatest commandment.

> One of them, a lawyer, asked Him a question, testing Him, "Teacher, which is the great commandment in the Law?" And He said to him, *'You shall love the Lord your God with all your heart, and with all your soul, and with all your mind.'* This is the great and foremost commandment. The second is like it, *'You shall love your neighbor as yourself.'* On these two commandments depend

the whole Law and the Prophets" (Matthew 22:35-40).

We each need to ask ourselves if we love Jesus. Do we love Jesus more than we love doing things for Jesus? Do we really live in such a way that demonstrates we fully trust Him for our right standing with God, or do we live with the nagging feeling that we are not good enough and are somehow second-class Christians? Do we really understand and apply God's grace to our entire life or just to our salvation? Do we truly realize our flawed condition (after salvation) and that we are in constant need of His love and forgiveness? Do we somehow delude ourselves and think we are "good" Christians and can do Christian things all on our own? Are we truly surprised when we fail and yet condemn ourselves because, after all, we should know better? One of the best ways to show your love for God is to completely trust Him for His grace and kindness regardless of your behavior.

At this point I want to say I am not advocating the heresy of libertarianism which is that people are free to live any way they please because they are forgiven due to their "faith" in Christ. Numerous are the commands and admonitions in the New Testament for holy living on the part of God's people. If your faith is destitute of good works, then you should seriously examine your claim of faith in Christ. Good works are confirmation of the presence of God's Spirit in a believer's life. With that said, let me point out something else. We as Christians will sin. We will miss the mark of God's perfect standard. Do not think otherwise. In the Sermon on the Mount Jesus pointed out that the invisible sins of the heart are just as heinous as outward visible sins when He equated lust with adultery and hate with murder. In fact, the invisible sins are probably the most egregious acts of mankind. No one can see lust, hate, selfishness, pride, indifference or lack of faith. We are all sinners even after salvation. Others may not see our sin, and we may not even see it, but God does. We can be thankful He is a very loving and patient Father who accepts us as we are and gently deals with our flaws. Once He points out a problem, our job is to look into our hearts, assess what's going on and turn away from the bad behavior or attitude. He will be revealing our hidden junk to us for as long as we live. Wonderfully, forgiveness is readily available, and our standing in Christ is secure for all of eternity. God's love and grace toward us are more relentless than we can imagine.

Let me quote Brennan Manning once more. "Since the day that Jesus first appeared on the scene, we have developed vast theological systems, organized worldwide churches, filled libraries with brilliant Christological scholarship, engaged in earthshaking controversies and embarked on crusades, reforms and renewals. Yet there are still precious few of us with sufficient folly to make the mad exchange of everything for Christ; only a remnant with the confidence to risk everything on the gospel of grace; only a minority who stagger about with the delirious joy of the man who found the buried treasure."[9]

If you are still clinging to your own efforts and are disappointed with your performance as a Christian, consider this: God expects more failure from us than we expect from ourselves.[10] Once this thought rattles through our souls and shatters the myth of self-sufficiency, we will again be reminded of God's goodness. We will want to abide in Him all the time because we realize just how needy we are. When we do abide in Him, good things can and will happen through us as the Holy Spirit is now able to live through us. This will make all the difference. Now we can do the same worthwhile Christian activities that once drained us of our vitality, but this time we are not alone. Also, when we recognize our needs and shortcomings, we should therefore be more compassionate and forgiving of others who fail or hurt us.

Killer bees work very hard and can accomplish good things quite effectively such as pollination and honey production. But they can be dangerous, and they do have a terrible reputation. As a point to ponder it should be noted that one researcher claims honeybees do rest. After foraging, a bee will crawl into an empty cell and be quiet for about a half hour.[11] Christians can accomplish good things, but if they work too hard for the wrong reasons they also can be dangerous to themselves and others as well as tarnish the cause of Christ. Be careful that you do not add to someone's load by suggesting they should do this or that. We are to bear one another's burden (Galatians 6:2), not add to it. Also do not let anyone shackle you with their checklist. Our standing in God's eyes as His precious child is secure despite our shortcomings. We need to pause and take time to rest in this fact. Reciprocate His love by loving Him and abiding in Him. Good things will happen.

Chapter 22

Being There

Bees, like every other creature on the planet, can experience severe hardships. Disease, parasites and unwanted intruders are not foreign to the honeybee world.

The American foul brood disease is the dread of every beekeeper. As the name implies, the disease affects the brood by turning the larvae into a lifeless sticky mass. There are preventive medicines but no cures. Once infected, the best course of action for the beekeeper is to seal the doomed bees inside the hive and place it in a hole in the ground and burn it. Although this sounds extreme, it is the most humane thing a beekeeper can do. If the beekeeper does nothing, the hive will weaken and eventually die anyway. While it is in decline, it will be the target of other honeybees who will seek to rob the sick hive. Robber bees can empty a weak hive of its honey in a matter of hours. When robbing a sick hive, however, the disease will be carried back to the robbers' hive. Therefore this disease can spread rapidly. Burning the hive will help destroy the bacterial spores which are the source of the disease. These spores have been known to lie dormant for fifty years[1] before coming to life to grow and claim more victims. So by destroying the stricken hive the beekeeper is ending the colony's suffering as well as sparing other colonies in his apiary, and any nearby colonies, from acquiring the disease.

The other diseases, such as European foul brood, sac brood, chalk brood and nosema, are not always fatal. They originate from some kind of harmful bacteria that enters the hive and wreaks varying degrees of havoc. These plagues are grouped together under the name of "stress diseases" and are attributable to a large extent on some external factor such as dampness; large temperature swings in the weather; excessive wind; limited nectar, pollen or water; or even impediments to the hive entrance. It is not uncommon for hives to be afflicted with several of these diseases simultaneously.[2] Most of these diseases can be treated with medication, or they can simply run their course and disappear from the hive.

These diseases are usually present in the springtime and can weaken the colony at this crucial time. A weakened colony will have an uphill struggle for the remainder of the year. A weak colony, one with a lower than normal population, will have trouble raising brood. The brood must be kept at a constant warm temperature to develop. With fewer bees in a hive there is a greater chance the brood will chill and die from cold springtime temperatures. With less brood surviving there will be fewer bees available in the next generation. As the outside temperature increases, the threat of chilled brood diminishes. If the population is not at full strength when the major nectar flow occurs, however, then the colony will forgo taking advantage of this large food supply. This food supply is largely what will sustain the colony during the coming winter.

Bees experience other hardships beside disease. They can be plagued by other insects. Yes, bugs bug other bugs. Varroa and tracheal mites hit with a vengeance in the United States in the mid 1980s. No one saw it coming. Numerous beekeepers were losing fifty percent or more of their hives during the winter. (Ten percent is a typical casualty rate for the winter.) The mites had infected the bees to such an extent that they could not survive the rigors of winter. The varroa mites sucked the life blood from the adults. They do more damage by cheating the developing brood of its food. The emerging bees are sickly and sometimes deformed, but more important they are of no use to the colony at a time when more healthy bodies mean more warmth for the hive in the winter. The tracheal mites live in the breathing tubes of the bees and can cause damage which can lead to infection. Many a bee would not return from a winter cleansing flight due to being in a weakened condition caused by the mites.

The mites were the result of breeding experiments that did not adequately anticipate the transfer of parasites from one species to another. The mites originally came from Asian honeybees. Asian bees are naturally resistant to the mites and their effects. The honeybees in North America, being of European descent, were basically defenseless. Once the mites became established in North America, commercial beekeepers hastened their spread as they transported their hives across the country to pollinate crops. Wild honeybees, as well as those kept by hobbyists, became infected by the mites. Left alone, hives will eventual die due to mite infestation. Therefore if one sees a honeybee on a flower in the backyard, it probably belongs to a local beekeeper that is treating his hive for mite infestation. Wild colonies of bees obviously receive no such treatment.

Once the problem of the mites was identified, various treatments and pesticides were employed to stop the mites and their effects. There is an ongoing biological war raging between scientists and the mites. A treatment is developed and deployed. Initially it will have an impact on most of the mites. But the surviving mites pass along their natural resistance to subsequent generations that can become more resistant to the treatments. The scientists would go back to the drawing board to come up with another toxin. The new treatment would show promising signs but would fail to completely eradicate the mites. These surviving mites develop a resistance to pass on to their offspring, and thus the war continues.

Beekeepers must employ an array of methods and treatments to control the mites. For example, some beekeepers will use a screened bottom board on their hives. Mites naturally fall off the bees and the comb. Instead of landing on a solid bottom board and crawling back up into the hive or on to another bee, the screen allows them to fall completely out of the hive, and thus there is a certain probability they will not return to the hive. Another method takes advantage of the varroa mites' natural inclination to target the brood of developing drones. Beekeepers may place one frame into the hive that has a foundation especially designed to build cells for raising drones. Once the cells are complete, the queen will lay eggs in them that develop into drones. (The queen knows which type of egg to lay —drone or worker—based upon the size of the cell.) Drone larvae tend to attract more mites. The workers will cap the drone cells for the final stage of development with the mites trapped inside. Once the cells are capped, the beekeeper will remove the frame from the hive and place it in a freezer. This will kill the concentrated collection of mites as well as the lazy undesired drones. The frame is placed back in the hive where the workers will remove the dead drones and mites so the process can be repeated.[3] Another method in fighting mites is to raise strains of honeybees naturally more resistant to the mites. Obviously, of course, there is the latest and greatest anti-mite drug. Beekeepers will usually use a combination of these methods in their fight against the mites.

The chemical treatments used to control the mites cause a bit of an inconvenience for beekeepers. Aside from the time, effort and expense involved, these treatments are toxic to humans. Therefore beekeepers need to take precautions when handling these pesticides. Also beekeepers must be careful when they apply these treatments. Boxes used to collect honey for human consumption cannot be placed upon a hive within a certain period of time after the treatment to avoid contaminating the honey.

Hive beetles are a more recent threat. They came from Africa and have no natural enemies in North America. The beetles will enter a hive and literally tunnel through the wax comb rupturing cells containing honey and brood alike. The result is a dripping gooey mess which causes the bees to abandon the hive. Treatments are available for the hive beetle. But because part of its life cycle is spent in sandy soil this pest is isolated to areas with this kind of soil. Beekeepers can prevent or minimize the hive beetle threat by placing their hives on solid bases so the hive beetles are deprived of a necessary element of their life cycle.

While I was in the final stages of finishing this book, a new honeybee plague was announced. Hives that appear to be healthy and strong one day are then completely empty of adult bees just a few days later. Some beekeepers are experiencing significant losses (about seventy-five percent) within their apiaries. Called *colony collapse disorder*, this condition is not well understood and could have a significant impact upon the pollination of certain crops within the United States.[4]

Wax moths, another unintended and undesired import, are a constant threat to a hive. A strong hive can easily defend itself and repel the moths. Weaker hives can be invaded by the moths. Once inside, the moths will lay eggs. When these eggs hatch, the moth larvae will eat the comb and leave a trail of feces and cobwebs. Before long, the moths will ruin the hive.

Mammals can also be a problem for bees. Mice like to enter the hive and make their winter nests there when the bees are dormant. The mice chew up relatively large amounts of comb to make room for their nests. The mice introduce dirt, debris and defecation into the otherwise sanitary hive. Skunks like to scratch at the hive entrance to irritate the bees. When the bees come out to investigate, the skunk will eat them about as fast as they appear. Despite the painful stings on the outside of its body, as well as on the inside, a skunk will remain undaunted in its dining. Bears wreak havoc on a grand scale. They will tear a hive apart to eat bees, brood and honey. They will continue their destructive ways until all of the hives in apiary are laid waste.[5]

We might as well add beekeepers to the list of problems the bees encounter. Someone said that once a beekeeper gets hooked on his hobby and cannot stay out of the hive he becomes the biggest threat to the bees. No matter how careful the beekeeper is, there will always be some casualties to the bees. Also, by separating the hive boxes and frames to conduct inspections, the beekeeper is undoing all the work the bees did to glue everything together. After the beekeeper leaves, the bees will re-glue everything and repair any damage done to the comb. This repair work will distract the bees from doing productive work such as rearing brood or gathering honey. It has been shown that a hive will gain twenty to thirty percent less weight on the day of an inspection as compared to hives that are not inspected.[6] There are two rules of thumb for beekeepers to consider.

One, it takes the bees about one day to recover from each entry a beekeeper makes into a hive. Two, a beekeeper should not spend more than ten hours a year in a hive.

As a beekeeper, I have suffered the loss of two hives from disease. One hive lasted four years before being killed by a disease, and the second died in its second season. Like most beekeepers, I was fond of my bees. I would quietly observe and admire their comings and goings from the hive. They would go about their chores with methodical efficiency. I would do all I could to ensure their well being by implementing the art of beekeeping to the best of my knowledge and ability. To control the mites, I treated them at the proper times of the year. I made sure they had a clear flight path into and out of their hive. I would keep my inspections to a minimum to respect their privacy and work. I would be thrilled at harvest time each year as I collected their excess honey. The golden liquid was something of which I was proud and very appreciative. I made sure they were in good shape going into the winter. During the winters I would quickly peek inside to check their remaining supplies. If I felt they were running short, I would make bee candy that I would place in the hive above their cluster so they would be sure to find it. Perhaps at times I was a little obsessive with how I doodled over my bees. Like a nervous parent I closely monitored their condition and would respond accordingly.

When I first detected that my hives were not well, I became sick at heart knowing there was nothing I could do to avert the inevitable. Although bees are not tamed like some animals and do not recognize or respond to their owners, the loss of a hive is a sad experience for any beekeeper. At my office there is a small group of beekeepers. We share stories about our bees like most people talk about their kids. Unfortunately each of us has experienced the loss of a hive due to one malady or another. We would express our sympathy to the one who had lost his hive knowing full well the sadness he was experiencing.

Why do hives perish? It seems tragic that a creature as industrious and beneficial as honeybees could experience what seems to be an unnecessary demise. From a scientific viewpoint the answer comes in the stoic fact that the rules of nature affect every living creature and none is exempt from the ebbs and flows of life's cycles of prosperity and demise. Although that is true, it is of little comfort to a beekeeper attached to his bees. Fortunately, time has a way of relieving the disappointment and enables us to forget and go forward.

Just as tragedy strikes a colony of bees in different ways to varying degrees, so we as followers of Christ experience severe loss and pain from events that seem so senseless and unnecessary. These tragic hardships can take many forms: the untimely or slow death of a close friend or family member, the loss of health or mobility due to a debilitating injury or accident, receiving news of a terminal disease, a marriage ending in divorce or, perhaps worst of all, a tragedy involving a child. The earlier chapter about winter focused upon the trying times in which God seemed to be silent or distant. This chapter is meant to address a major crisis of faith caused by acute tragedy. None of us is immune. Inevitably we will all experience at least one of these faith-shaking events in our lives. From a broken and confused heart we will cry out to God asking, "Why?!"

Personally I have experienced some of these tragedies. My father, a devoted family man, died of lymphoma at the young age of fifty-three just as I was starting to get to know him man-to-man. During that same year my father-in-law experienced a major heart attack and a debilitating stroke. It was heart wrenching to see a once strong and independent man relying on others in his final months for basic care and necessities. After dealing with the loss of our fathers, my wife and I came to grips with the sobering fact that we could not have children. Dreams of being parents with family vacations and holidays meals around the table were shattered. Worst of all, the reminder of our childless condition would always manifest itself anytime we went out into public and saw young families or passed a toy store. More recently, I experienced a direct hit when I was diagnosed with melanoma. I will never forget the initial fear of hearing the diagnosis and experiencing the mental anguish of wondering if my procrastination of getting a checkup would cost me my life. One of the most difficult things about my experience with melanoma was I had just finished seminary only two months before I received my diagnosis. I thought God had big plans for me and would use me and my new degree for years to come. Somehow I thought I was going to be immune from personal tragedies at least until I was quite old. "Why," I thought, "would God strike me with cancer?"

The question of why tragedies and evil in general exist in the world is a thorny one for Christians to answer. The question usually appears in this form: If God is all-loving and all-knowing and all-powerful, why can't He just eliminate evil and horrible things from the world? The conclusion that skeptics reach usually goes something like this: Since evil and tragedies exist in the world, then God is not all-loving, all-knowing or all-powerful; or He does not exist at all. Nonbelievers usually sit smugly nestled in their logical fortress rationalizing their existence apart from moral and spiritual accountability as they wait to taunt the next Christian who comes along. Christians, especially those who have experienced extreme hardships, also ponder this dilemma. Christians who dwell too long on this can poison their souls with bitterness toward God as they feel betrayed by Someone they thought they could trust.

I believe there are reasonable responses to this issue that Christians should consider and understand.[7] Depending upon the person and the situation, some explanations may be more helpful than others. But the effort here is not to explain the problem of evil. Instead it is to try to explain why some Christians, or people in general, struggle so deeply when dealing with tragedy. First off, let it be said it is okay to experience pain and to grieve deeply as a result of encountering significant hardships. It is also okay to doubt God and wrestle with Him over these things. You do not need to lie by painting a fake smile on your face and saying you are fine when deep down you know you are at the end of your rope. Second, let it be stated that this explanation of why prolonged struggling occurs will not make anyone feel any better while in the midst of a terrible hardship. A wounded heart is only something God can mend in His time and His way. The explanation below is simply intended to cause people to examine their own hearts when they are unable or unwilling to get past a horrible experience and their faith has been crippled.

Whenever anyone makes an assertion of any kind, he or she is basing that assertion on some underlying premise. For this issue I believe that when someone cannot get over, or work through, a tragedy after significant time has passed, there are probably two underlying premises.

The first premise is that we are operating under the false assumption that this life in the body is all there is. Christians will immediately object to this because they will claim heaven awaits them after death. This is true. But how many of us live our lives with this truth in the forefront of our minds? If we are honest with ourselves, we will have to confess that we, especially in Western culture, are more attached to this world and our own lives than we would like to admit. Consider how you spend your time and your money. How much of your time is devoted to things of eternal value or trying to convince others that eternal life can be theirs? I am not trying to lay a guilt trip on anyone, but do you get more excited about going to a ballgame or a family reunion than doing something that expands God's kingdom? Now look at your checkbook. Compare the money you spend on leisure and investing to the money you give to support God's work. Do you even have a will drawn up to disperse some or all of your estate to worthy Christian ministries when you die? After all, you cannot take it with you. Furthermore, if you could take it with you, it would not be worth much in a place where the streets are paved with gold (Revelation 21:21). Although we as Christians claim heaven as our ultimate home, we tend to live our lives as if heaven were really not there. I am not against ballgames, family reunions, leisure or investments. All I am pointing out is that we need to be more aware of the true attitudes and values in our hearts and how they play out in our lives.

The heart is a mysterious place. It is the location of the truest you. There is a throne in your heart. Who is sitting on it? God? You? Something or someone else? One way I monitor what is going on in my heart is by reflecting upon how I have reacted to various things or situations. For instance, if someone cuts me off in traffic just to get one car length ahead of me and I get seriously upset and offended, then I probably have pride or self on the throne in my heart. Really, what will it matter one hundred years from now if I am delayed by a half second by someone cutting me off in traffic?

I cannot control the driving habits of other drivers, but I can control how I react. Angrily honking my horn is not a good witness for Christ, nor is it pleasing to Him when I have hate or animosity toward a complete stranger for what is really a very minor infraction. When I realize my reactions are wrong, I then must assess what is going on in my heart. Obviously I must be holding myself in higher esteem than I should if I let another driver evoke such a strong negative reaction from me. Why this type of reaction? When something which we value is threatened (such as *self* in this example), we will react strongly. By placing an inappropriate value on something we have made it an idol or false god in our lives. When we do this we are violating the first commandment: You shall have no other gods before Me (Exodus 20:3).

Reflect upon instances in which you have had a strong reaction to someone or some event. What idol was threatened in your heart? You may be surprised at what you will find.

Going back to the first premise, we need to be aware of our true attitudes and values that we have concerning our lives and the things in our lives. In an earlier chapter I discussed how transient we really are. A long quiet walk through a cemetery will remind us that our lives here on earth, and all the things in our lives, are truly just specks of dust which briefly appear and then disappear in light of eternity. When we allow ourselves to think we have to get as much gusto out of this life as possible before it is over, then we have bought into the world's values. Jesus said, "For where your treasure is, there your heart will be also" (Matthew 6:21). Where is your treasure? What is your treasure? Having false gods on the throne of our hearts causes us to hold on tightly to things which we should not. When we hang on to things or people more tightly than we should, it will always hurt much more than it should when that thing or person is taken from us than if we had had a loose grip. Only God deserves to be seated upon the throne of our hearts. He is eternal. He will not go away. We can hold tightly to Him.

The second premise is that we somehow think God exists to serve us. This thought probably seems ridiculous. But answer this: Have you ever seen anyone raise their fist in anger toward heaven and curse God for all the *good* things in their life? I have not, and I doubt anyone ever has. Why? We all hope things in life will go well. We do not buy a new car hoping it will be turned into a mass of twisted metal. We do not plant gardens so only weeds will sprout. We do not spend years working to turn a house into a home so that later it will burn to the ground. We do not get married so we can experience infidelity and divorce. We do not invest to lose money. We do not go to school to get dumber. Whatever we do we hope it is successful. We hope God blesses us and makes good things happen in our lives.

During our exertions at bettering our lot in life, we as Christians and even many non-Christians alike realize God is watching over us and could unimaginably bless us if He chose to do so. Health, wealth and prosperity preachers will show us verses from the Bible that seem to guarantee a blessed life. At the very least we have all heard at one time or another that God will take care of us. So as we travel down life's road we hope for a big promotion, a large inheritance, a perfect spouse, a long healthy life or even to win the lottery. When these things do not happen we then resign ourselves to admitting it was just not God's will. We then disappointedly trudge on with our lives. Then when tragedy strikes, this disappointment with God can quickly turn to rage. Just as He did not seem interested enough to intervene to make our lives better He likewise did not insert Himself to protect us from being afflicted with some awful tragedy.

Admittedly, from our perspective, things do not always seem fair. I have known people who have made great sacrifices in their lives to serve God as their full-time vocation. While in the midst of their service, though, they encounter one seemingly needless obstacle or setback after another. Some of these people have suffered serious illnesses, or their children have been chronically ill. Some have even died. Jesus addressed His disciples saying, "The harvest is plentiful, but the workers are few. Therefore beseech the Lord of the harvest to send out workers into His harvest" (Matthew 9:37-38). It almost seems ludicrous that when His people are following His directive to gather the harvest He would allow them to encounter such awful struggles. One day we will find out what God was orchestrating amidst all of these heartaches. But for now we must go on.

We all must admit we have thought at one time or another that by making a big sacrifice for the Lord we should somehow be entitled to an extra blessing or layer of protection. The truth is we are not entitled to anything. Yet many Christians live their lives under an equation that goes something like this: Becoming a Christian + Serving Christ = Blessings. I once heard a Christian counselor share an interesting point. He said most people in mental institutions claim to be Christians. If that is true, I cannot help but wonder if those Christians tried to live their lives according to the above equation and simply snapped when the reality of tragedy touched their lives for no apparent reason. Without trying to sound like a cliché, God's ways are mysterious to us. Yes, we are to hold on to His promises, but we are not to presume our will upon Him. Even in the Garden of Gethsemane Jesus prayed, "My Father, if it is possible, let this cup pass from Me; yet not as I will, but as You will" (Matthew 26:39). We are to serve God to accomplish His plans. He does not serve us to accomplish our plans.

To recap, the two erroneous premises are our perspective about the things of this life and God being our servant. Written like this, almost every Christian would vehemently deny such assertions. But when we truly examine our hearts and our perspective of God we may realize these two premises are closer to the truth than we would like to admit. As humans we will never be perfect. We will always be refining our understanding and application of the truths of Scripture. We can be thankful God is patient with us and knows we are weak in so many ways. He expects more failure from us than we do of ourselves. He uses trials, minor and major, to make us "perfect and complete, lacking in nothing" (James 1:2-4). Again, these words and the above explanation cannot lessen the pain of an overwhelming loss or tragedy. They are only meant as food for thought when considering what may be going on in our hearts.

How does all this relate to the bees? Everything the bees do is for the benefit of the entire colony. They do whatever needs to be done whenever it is needed. They are there for each other. They do not say a word; they are simply there for each.

One time during my beekeeping experience I saw something I would not have believed if I had not seen it myself. It was something I shall never forget either. Just as with previous inspections of my hive I would first smoke the bees to calm them. Sometimes the smoker worked better than other times, and this was one such time. As usual the bees fled to escape the thick smoke. After I finished my inspection and had reassembled the hive, I noticed some bees were partially sticking out of a crack on the back side of the hive between two lower sections of the hive. This crack was a few inches in length but not wide enough to allow the bees to pass through completely. Thus, about five or six bees were wedged in this crack with their heads sticking out of the back of the hive. They evidently had tried to escape from the smoke by attempting to fit through this crack. I remember deciding to let them alone because I would end up killing more bees by disassembling and reassembling the hive in order to try to free these few bees. Furthermore, since they had gotten themselves into that jam, I figured they could get themselves out of it.

A week went by before I returned to my hive. I remembered to look at the back of the hive to see if those bees had freed themselves. All but one was free. I truly felt bad for the poor bee that had been confined there by herself for a whole week wedged in the crack with her head exposed to the elements during the long days and nights. While staring in pity at this bee, I saw another bee fly around to the back of the hive to visit her stuck sister. It appeared she was feeding her! My guilt from leaving the bee stuck there for a week was compounded by the compassion shown by her sister.

I was absolutely amazed at this on three counts. One, I had never seen bees flying around to the back side of a hive except during an inspection when the hive was apart and the bees were disoriented. There is simply no reason for them to go back there. Two, I had never read anything about bees trying to rescue or help stricken comrades; therefore I was seeing something rare. Three, most of what bees do is driven by instinct or pheromones. Seeing this one bee go to the back of the hive and come to the aid of another bee seemed to demonstrate that consciousness, on some level, was taking place within the bee's mere one milligram of brain matter.[8]

The stuck bee was simply at the wrong place at the wrong time when I applied the smoke to the hive on the day I conducted my inspection. If I had applied the smoke a few seconds earlier or later, that bee would have been in another location inside the hive away from the crack, or she may not have even been in the hive at all. Once she realized she was stuck she may have asked herself, "Why am I trapped? What did I do to deserve this? Am I going to die?" Coming to grips with her entrapment would not have been an easy thing to do. One minute she was free to fly about, and the next she was trapped. There was nothing she could do to change her situation. There was nothing her sixty thousand sisters could do to change her situation either.

We can learn one thing from this account of the visiting bee. Although powerless to free her sister she did what she could do. She provided basic necessities and the presence of her company. When we, or people around us, are in the midst of a terrible situation we would like nothing more than to be able to make the trial to go away. But we cannot. We can do other things, though. Like the visiting bee, we can ensure that those who are suffering or grieving have their basic needs met and let them know they are not alone. When with them we should be slow to speak. Our presence is the best gift we can give as words usually ring hollow and can many times be very irritating. If we have suffered in a similar way, then maybe we can share, at the prompting of the Holy Spirit, the comfort God gave us when we were suffering. Paul wrote, "Blessed be the God and Father of our Lord Jesus Christ, the Father of mercies and God of all comfort, who comforts us in all our affliction so that we will be able to comfort those who are in any affliction with the comfort with which we ourselves are comforted by God" (2 Corinthians 1:3-4). Simply being there with someone can sometimes be the best comfort of all.

Do not try to dwell too long on answering the deep "Why?" questions of life. Perhaps the answer will be revealed in time. I was fortunate regarding my melanoma. It was only stage one and was isolated to a single spot, and I had it removed. Perhaps other times the answers to our questions will never be known. As mortals we must accept our limitations, especially our ability to understand why things happen as they do. Perhaps the best verse I have found when pondering life's deep questions is Deuteronomy 29:29 which says, "The secret things belong to the Lord our God, but the things revealed belong to us and to our sons forever, that we may observe all the words of this law." God reveals only certain things to us. The rest belongs to Him.

God is there with us in our darkest hour. He promised never to leave us or forsake us (Hebrews 13:5). Perhaps we can reflect this characteristic of His image in the world by simply being there for others during their time of tragedy.

Chapter 23

Navigation

Honeybees are excellent navigators. They can orient themselves based upon the position of the sun. They also have a remarkable capability to measure distance when flying. They combine the skills of determining direction and distance while factoring in detours around large objects such as buildings or hills. They can even traverse valleys and factor in elevation changes. Furthermore, because they have iron deposits in their bodies, scientists report that bees can detect and use the earth's magnetic field to aid in their navigational process.[1]

Despite all these amazing capabilities there are strange limitations to a bee's navigational skills. It has been said that if you are going to move a beehive it must be moved either less than three feet or more than three miles.[2] In other words, if one moves a beehive more than three feet but less than three miles, then the bees after leaving the hive will return to the original location of the hive. Perhaps this phenomenon occurs as a result of the bees repeating the same navigational maneuvers when flying around the area of the hive and possibly recognizing landmarks of the countryside. Hives used commercially for pollination are moved hundreds of miles between stops as they follow the springtime blossoms. Evidently when the bees arrive at a completely new site well removed from their previous location they reset their little GPS systems and start from scratch. The bees adapt immediately and carry on with business as usual after a big move.

An interesting observation can be seen, however, when one moves a hive about ten feet. When the foraging bees return to the hive they will return to the original location even though their home is easily visible being only several feet away.[3] Beekeepers use this to their advantage on occasion. For example, if the beekeeper is trying to find the queen, he will move the hive about ten or twelve feet. He will do this in the middle of the day when a large part of the workforce is out foraging for food. The beekeeper will leave an empty super in the location of the original hive so the returning bees will at least have some place to hang out (all the while they will be wondering if they took a wrong turn somewhere during the trip home or if they flew through the Bermuda Triangle). With the hive in its new location it will be a little easier for the beekeeper to find the queen with thousands fewer worker bees filling the hive. When the beekeeper is finished he will move the hive back to its original location and shake the bees out of the empty super onto the ground in front of the hive. From there they will find their way back up into the hive and continue with their chores.

Regardless of this quirky phenomenon a honeybee's navigational skills are absolutely necessary for survival of the individual as well as for the entire colony. If an individual bee cannot find its way home, it will eventually die of exposure. If the bees cannot reliably navigate to and from a food source, then the brood in the colony will starve as foragers will not consistently return with food. Just as the bees must utilize their navigational skills to survive, Christians must rely on God's guidance to live full and meaningful lives as individuals as well as members of a body of believers.

In Scripture we have numerous examples of God leading people by various means and with varying degrees of specificity. Adam and Eve were forced out of the Garden of Eden (Genesis 3:23). Abraham was simply told to get up and go (Genesis 12:1). Joseph, wrongfully thrown into an Egyptian prison, was rescued and made pharaoh's right-hand man because he could interpret dreams (Genesis 41:40). Moses encountered a burning bush (Exodus 3:4). The Israelites had a pillar of cloud by day and fire by night (Exodus 13:21). Balaam was told by a donkey to stop before he was about to be killed by an angel (Numbers 22:28). Gideon did his thing by way of confirmation through a wet and dry fleece (Judges 6:36-40). David had a prophet show up and anoint him (1 Samuel 16:13). It took a great fish to put Jonah back on track (Jonah 2:10). The magi followed a star (Matthew 2:2, 9). Joseph, Jesus' earthly guardian, was directed through dreams to move his family from one place to another (Matthew 2:13, 19, 22). The eleven apostles drew lots to pick a replacement for Judas (Acts 1:26). Then came Pentecost (Acts 2).

Shortly before Jesus' arrest He told His disciples the Father would send the Helper (John 14:16). Jesus was referring to the Holy Spirit. Jesus told His disciples the Holy Spirit would indwell them (vv. 16-17), teach them (v. 26) and help them recall His words (v. 26). At Pentecost in Acts 2 the Holy Spirit was poured out upon His followers just as He had promised. The Spirit arrived with the sound of a mighty rushing wind filling the house where Christ's followers were huddled together. Then flaming tongues appeared and rested upon each one. They were filled with the Spirit and were speaking in foreign languages. This caused quite a ruckus in the town and caught the attention of many. Peter, who had succumbed to fear and denied Christ just a few weeks earlier, arose with boldness and confidence to address the crowd. Through the Spirit's work, Peter's preaching resulted in three thousand souls being added to the church that day. What follows in the book of Acts are numerous miraculous accounts of the work of the Holy Spirit through these first-century believers.

When one reads Acts, one can be amazed and somewhat intimidated by the works of the Spirit. Sometimes it almost seems like the working of God's Spirit is something that only happened long ago through special people. But God's Spirit is active throughout the world today and is working through His church in various ways. The role of the Holy Spirit in the life of the believer is vital. The Greek word *paraclete* is what John used when writing about the Holy Spirit (John 14:16, 26). Concepts associated with this Greek word include consoling, admonishing, exhorting and persuading. The Spirit does many things to help believers. But for here it is the Spirit's role in leading or guiding believers that is of interest.

Unfortunately today a lot of controversy surrounds the role of the Holy Spirit in the life of a believer. Some believers hold to a demonstrative role of the Spirit whereas others embrace a more subdued personal role, and of course there are those in between these two positions. Each camp has a basis for its position. We will only know for certain who was more correct when we get to heaven. But there is a lot of living to do before we get to heaven. Hopefully our time here on earth can be productive and meaningful as we seek to expand God's kingdom and bring honor to Him. We will need the help of the Helper to live full and abundant lives for the sake of the King. We need to let the Holy Spirit take charge of our lives.

Paul issued a command to believers in Ephesians 5:18—"Be filled with the Spirit." This command indicates a few things. First, because Paul had to issue the command it can be reasonably implied that being *filled* with the Spirit is something that does not automatically happen for believers. Believers receive the Spirit when they come to trust Christ as their Savior and Lord (Ephesians 1:13). At salvation it can be said that believers are *indwelt* with the Holy Spirit. Although the Spirit is indwelling each believer, the Spirit may not be filling or controlling each believer and thus the reason for Paul's command. Second, a command is something to obey or not. Believers have a choice as to whether or not to be filled with the Spirit. So the issue really is not so much about getting more of the Holy Spirit but letting the Holy Spirit get more of you.

What does it mean to be filled with the Spirit? Paul prefaced this command by warning believers not to get drunk with wine. The alcohol in wine can exert influence and cause a person to lose control. Thus, being filled with the Spirit is being influenced and yielded to God's control. It is allowing Him to set your agenda, change your values and empower you to do His work. It involves a deep-seated trust to keep His commands while living in a world hostile to the things of God. Being filled with the Spirit also entails constantly abiding in Him (John 15:4). One should not segregate life into the spiritual and secular. In other words one should not act, think or talk differently on Sunday morning at church than during the rest of the week. Abiding is literally a moment-by-moment reliance and connectedness with God through prayer. It is difficult to go astray if you are continuously communicating with Him at the heart level. First Thessalonians 5:17 says "pray without ceasing." The word translated *without ceasing* is used to describe a hacking cough.[4] This verse means to be in an attitude of constant prayer, not just during selected worship or devotional times.[5]

Many people in America claim to be Christians. Despite this claim there are numerous problems. The divorce rate lingers around fifty percent. Parents and children are estranged from one another. Kids, who cannot read, graduate from high school. Substance abuse abounds. When no one is looking, short cuts in tax preparations occur because, after all, "everybody else does it." Homelessness and hopelessness plague big and small cities alike while those in affluent suburbs engage in the petty game of "keeping up with the Joneses." The entertainment industry continues to dull our morals by pushing the envelope of acceptability. Politicians and judges enact or uphold outrageous laws while getting away with significant moral lapses with barely an objection from an apathetic public. The once trusted clergy are now feared to be pedophiles. Rich or poor, young or old, blue collar or white, urban or suburban, educated or not, our whole society is deteriorating. Where is the influence of the many so-called Christians? It is the humble opinion of the author that the reason for the impotence of the American church is directly attributable to the failure of believers to be filled with God's Spirit and constantly abiding in Him. The result is a weak and sickly witness to a world in dire need of God's help, love and forgiveness. I too often must include myself among the ranks of believers who fail to continually yield to God's Spirit.

Perhaps one reason for this individual weakness in believers is the lack of listening. Prayer is not just talking *to* God but talking *with* God. It is a two-way communication. How many of us pause during our prayer times to listen? Psalm 46:10 says, "Cease striving and know that I am God; I will be exalted among the nations, I will be exalted in the earth."

The American lifestyle is one continual striving after one thing or another. We are driving ourselves into the ground.

Even Jesus made it a point to get alone and pray. This need for solitude and prayer in His life must have been very significant as it is recorded in all four Gospels (Matthew 14:23, Mark 6:46, Luke 9:18 and John 6:15). If Jesus needed to get away to a quiet spot, who do we think we are if we do not do the same?

Elijah the prophet had an interesting encounter with God. "So He said, 'Go forth and stand on the mountain before the Lord.' And behold, the Lord was passing by! And a great and strong wind was rending the mountains and breaking in pieces the rocks before the Lord; but the Lord was not in the wind. And after the wind an earthquake, but the Lord was not in the earthquake. After the earthquake a fire, but the Lord was not in the fire; and after the fire a sound of a gentle blowing. When Elijah heard it, he wrapped his face in his mantle and went out and stood in the entrance of the cave. And behold, a voice came to him and said, 'What are you doing here, Elijah?'" (1 Kings 19:11-13).

The Lord performed a "shock and awe campaign" for Elijah. Despite the powerful acts of wind, earthquake and fire God was not there. He manifested Himself through *a gentle blowing* which the King James Bible translates as a *still small voice*. With all the awesome displays of power that had occurred on that mountain it would be interesting to know how long the Lord was whispering before Elijah finally heard Him. Can we hear this *still small voice* today with all we have going on around us? Are the ears of our heart attuned to His voice? It is interesting to note in the Gospel of John, when Jesus is first referring to the Spirit, He likens the Spirit to the wind. "The wind blows where it wishes and you hear the sound of it, but do not know where it comes from and where it is going; so is everyone who is born of the Spirit" (John 3:8).

The precise navigation of the honeybee is as much a fascination as it is a mystery. The bees use the sun, magnetic fields and landmarks to find their way. But internal to the bee is a mysterious process that integrates the data to get the bee to its destination. The inner workings of the heart of man are likewise mysterious as it relates to God. In seeking God's guidance many believers often look for external signs, such as events or circumstances. Sometimes they are obvious, but many times they are not. Perhaps we are *looking* in the wrong place for the answer. The answer may be in a still small voice that is as subtle as a gentle breeze. All we may need to do is just *listen.*

NOTES

Chapter 1 The Body and the Bees
1. John Calvin, *Commentary on the Epistle of Paul the Apostle to the Corinthians Volume 1*, trans. John Pringle (Grand Rapids, Michigan: William B. Eerdmans Publishing Company, 1948), p. 398.
2. Archibald Thomas Robertson, *Word Pictures in the New Testament, Volume IV: The Epistles of Paul* (Nashville, Tennessee: Broadman Press, 1931), pp. 170-171.
3. John MacAuthur, *The MacAuthur New Testament Commentary, 1 Corinthians* (Chicago, Illinois: The Moody Bible Institute, 1984), pp. 290-291.
4. Kenneth L. Chafin, *The Communicator's Commentary Series, Volume 7: 1,2 Corinthians*; ed. Lloyd J. Ogilvie (Waco, Texas: Word Books, 1985), p. 151.
5. MacAuthur, p. 318.
6. Roger A. Morse, *The New Complete Guide to Beekeeping* (Woodstock, Vermont: The Countryman Press, 1994), p. 168.

Chapter 2 The Basics of Bees
1. Morse, p. 11.
2. Dewey M. Caron, *Honey Bee Biology and Beekeeping* (Cheshire, Connecticut: Wicwas Press, 1999), p. 277.
3. William Longgood, *The Queen Must Die* (New York, New York: W. W. Norton & Company, 1985), p. 228.
4. Caron, p. 39.
5. Morse, p. 21.
6. *Ibid.*, p. 17.

Chapter 3 A Good Foundation

1. Caron, p. 263.
2. *Starting Right with Bees: A Beginner's Handbook on Beekeeping, 18th Edition;* The Editorial Staff of Gleanings in Bee Culture (Medina, Ohio: The A. I. Root Company, Publishers, 1976) p. 20.
3. Morse, p. 146.
4. Longgood, pp. 66-67.
5. Ibid.
6. Morse, p. 23.

Chapter 4 The Nursery

1. Longgood, pp. 78-79.
2. Morse, p. 20.
3. Caron, p. 42.
4. Morse, p. 168.
5. Harold Shelly, lecturing at Biblical Theological Seminary for the course NT/TH 705J-Px, The Theology of James and Peter, Fall Semester, 2003.

Chapter 5 Cleaning House

1. Morse, p. 158.
2. *Ibid.*, p. 113.
3. Craig Keener, *The InterVarsity Press Bible Background Commentary: New Testament* (Downers Grove, Illinois: InterVarsity Press, 1993), p. 508.
4. Charles Caldwell Ryrie, *Ryrie Study Bible: Expanded Edition* (Chicago: Moody Press, 1995), p. 1378.
5. Keener, p. 487.

Chapter 6 The Center of Attention

1. Caron, p. 45.
2. *Ibid.*, p. 104.
3. *Starting Right with Bees*, p. 37.
4. *Ibid.*, p. 11.
5. Caron, p. 103.

6. Harold Shelly, lecturing at Biblical Theological Seminary for the course NT/TH 705J-Px, The Theology of James and Peter, Fall Semester, 2003.

Chapter 7 Drones
1. Morse, p. 164.
2. *Ibid.*, p. 173.
3. Caron, pp. 120-121.
4. Longgood, p. 161.
5. Ryrie, p. 1562.
6. D. A. Carson, Douglas J. Moo, and Leon Morris; *An Introduction to the New Testament* (Grand Rapids, Michigan: Zondervan, 1992), p. 352.

Chapter 8 Communications
1. Caron, pp. 89-101.
2. *Ibid.*, p. 100.
3. *Ibid.*, p. 328.
4. *Ibid.*, pp. 79-81.
5. Longgood, p. 85.
6. Caron, p. 80.

Chapter 9 Personal Business
1. Morse, p. 103.
2. *Ibid.*, pp. 121-122.
3. Ryrie, p. 1523.

Chapter 10 Guard Bees
1. Morse, p. 17.
2. Longgood, p. 177.
3. Morse, p. 161.
4. Caron, pp. 41, 46.
5. Morse, p. 171.
6. Keener, p. 635.

Chapter 11 Thieves
1. Longgood, p. 212.
2. *Starting Right with Bees*, p. 56.

Chapter 12 Belonging

1. Brennan Manning, *The Ragamuffin Gospel* (Sisters, Oregon: Multnomah Publishers Inc., 2005), p. 27.
2. T. Desmond Alexander et al., New Dictionary of Biblical Theology (Downers Grove, Illinois: InterVarsity Press, 2000), pp. 525, 527.
3. C. S. Lewis, *Mere Christianity* (New York, New York: Macmillan Publishing Co., 1952), p. 56.
4. Class notes from Robert C. Newman for TH 655 Evidence of the Christian Faith; Winter Term, 2003, Biblical Theological Seminary; referencing David G. Meyers, "The Inflated Self," *Christian Century* (1 Dec 1982), pp. 1226-1230.
5. Ryrie, p. 1971.
6. George Eldon Ladd, *A Theology of the New Testament* (Grand Rapids, Michigan: William B. Eerdmans Publishing Company, 1993), p. 639.
7. Harold Shelly, lecturing at Biblical Theological Seminary for the course NT/TH 705J-Px, The Theology of James and Peter, Fall Semester, 2003.
8. Ryrie, p. 1795.

Chapter 13 Honey

1. Caron, p. 241.
2. *Starting Right with Bees*, p. 75.
3. Longgood, p. 195.
4. Caron, p. 240.
5. Morse, p. 112.
6. *Starting Right with Bees,* p. 78, citing a report in *Gazette Apicole*.
7. Caron, p. 7.
8. Morse, p. 36.
9. Caron, pp. 3-4.
10. Morse, pp. 130, 151.
11. Caron, p. 262.
12. Ryrie, p. 1558.
13. Lee Strobel, *The Case for Christ* (Grand Rapids, Michigan: Zondervan, 1998), pp. 81, 101-110.

14. F. F. Bruce, *The Canon of Scripture* (Downers Grove, Illinois: InterVarsity Press, 1988).

Chapter 14 Winter of the Soul
1. Caron, p. 214.
2. *Starting Right with Bees*, pp. 59-64.

Chapter 15 Mutiny
1. Longgood, pp. 54, 122-124.
2. *Starting Right with Bees*, p. 43.
3. Caron, pp. 106, 129.

Chapter 16 Smoke
1. Ryrie, p. 2070.

Chapter 17 Stuck on You
1. Morse, p. 113.
2. Caron, p. 69.
3. Henry T. Blackaby and Claude V. King, *Experiencing God* (Nashville, Tennessee: LifeWay Press, 1990), p. 8.
4. Brennan Manning, *Ruthless Trust* (New York: HarperCollins Publishing Inc., 2000), pg. 57.
5. Caron, p. 144.
6. Manning, *The Ragamuffin Gospel*, p. 158.

Chapter 18 Influencing Your World
1. Caron, pp. 163, 322.
2. Morse, p. 139.
3. *Ibid.*, p. 20.
4. *Ibid.*, pp. 138-139.
5. Caron, pp. 276-277.
6. Henry H. Halley, *Halley's Bible Handbook: New Revised Edition*, 23rd Edition (Grand Rapids, Michigan: Regency Reference Library from Zondervan Publishing House, 1962), p. 802.
7. Robert C. Newman lecture notes for Evidence for the Christian Faith, Winter Term, 2003, Biblical Theological Seminary; referencing Luis Bush, "Getting to the Core of

the Core: The 10/40 Window," Partners International, 1470 N 4th, San Jose, CA 95112.
8. Clarence Hall, "What I Found at Shimmabuke," *American Bible Society: The Record*, Vol. 95, No. 3. p. 58, April 1950.

Chapter 19 Multiplication by Division
1. *Starting Right with Bees*, p. 51.
2. Morse, p. 71.
3. Caron, p. 110.
4. Morse, p. 65.
5. Longgood, pp. 133-134.
6. Morse, p. 168.
7. Keener, p. 74.

Chapter 20 Cutting Edge
1. Morse, pp. 170-171.
2. Sandia National Laboratories News Release, April 27, 1999; *Sandia, University of Montana Researchers Try Training Bees to Find Buried Landmines.*
3. *Ibid.*
4. *Ibid.*
5. Peter Cohn, "Defense Bill Includes Funding for Landmine Detection Bees," *CongressDaily*, August 3, 2006.
6. *Ibid.*
7. For more on postmodernism see: Stanley J. Getz, A *Primer on Postmodernism*, Wm. B. Eerdmans Publishing Company, 1996; and D.A. Carson, Becoming *Conversant with the Emergent Church*, Zondervan, 2005

Chapter 21 Killer Bees
1. Caron, p. 21.
2. Much of the information in this chapter about African bees is from Roger A. Morse, pp. 179-188.
3. Gregory Juckett and John G. Hancox, "Venomous Snakebites in the United States: Management Review and Update," *American Family Physician*, Vol. 65, No. 7, April 1, 2002.
4. Caron, pp. 167, 169.

5. Manning, p. 40.
6. Taken from: Classic Christianity by Bob George, Copyright © 2000 by Harvest House Publishers, Eugene, OR. Used by Permission. www.harvesthousepublishers.com
7. John Eldredge, *Wild at Heart* (Nashville, Tennessee: Thomas Nelson Publishers, 2001), p. 172.
8. Manning, pp. 16-17.
9. *Ibid.,* pp. 201-202.
10. *Ibid.,* p. 174.
11. Longgood, p. 94.

Chapter 22 Being There
1. *Starting Right with Bees*, p, 89.
2. Morse, pp. 118-119.
3. *Brushy Mountain Bee Farm 2006 Catalog of Beekeeper Supplies* (Brushy Mountain Bee Farm Inc., 610 Bethany Church Road, Moravian Falls, North Carolina 28654), p. 29.
4. Wikipedia.org/wiki/Colony_Collapse_Disorder
5. Morse, pp. 125-126.
6. Caron, p. 193.
7. For a good explanation of the problem of evil, I would recommend W. Gary Phillips and William E. Brown, *Making Sense of Your World from a Biblical Viewpoint* (Chicago, Illinois: Moody Press, 1991), pp. 133-157.
8. Longgood, p. 61.

Chapter 23 Navigation
1. Caron, pp. 55, 85-86.
2. Morse, p. 154.
3. Caron, pp. 198-199.
4. Ryrie, p. 1910.
5. Keener, p. 595.

Printed in the United States
81950LV00001B/106-300